teaching and learning

Japanese Martial Arts

scholarly perspectives

An Anthology of Articles
from the *Journal of Asian Martial Arts*
Compiled by Michael A. DeMarco, M.A.

Disclaimer

Please note that the authors and publisher of this book are not responsible in any manner whatsoever for any injury that may result from practicing the techniques and/or following the instructions given within. Since the physical activities described herein may be too strenuous in nature for some readers to engage in safely, it is essential that a physician be consulted prior to training.

All Rights Reserved

No part of this publication, including illustrations, may be reproduced or utilized in any form or by any means, electronic or mechanical, including photocopying, recording, or by any information storage and retrieval system (beyond that copying permitted by sections 107 and 108 of the US Copyright Law and except by reviewers for the public press), without written permission from Via Media Publishing Company.

Warning: Any unauthorized act in relation to a copyright work may result in both a civil claim for damages and criminal prosecution.

Copyright © 2017
by Via Media Publishing Company
941 Calle Mejia #822, Santa Fe, NM 87501 USA

Articles in this anthology were originally published in the *Journal of Asian Martial Arts*. Listed according to the table of contents for this anthology:

Harrison-Pepper, S. (1993). Vol. 2 No. 2, pp. 90-103
Monday, N. (1994). Vol. 3 No. 1, pp. 72-89
Hershey, L. (1994). Vol. 3 No. 3, pp. 52-61
Varley, P. (1995). Vol. 4 No. 4, pp. 10-11
Hurst, G. C. (1995). Vol. 4 No. 4, pp. 12-25
Friday, C. (1995). Vol. 4 No. 4, pp. 26-39
VanHorne, W. (1996). Vol. 5 No. 4, pp. 10-19
Donohue, J. (2005). Vol. 14 No. 2, pp. 8-29
Donohue, J. (2006). Vol. 15 No. 3, pp. 8-19
Taylor, K. (2009). Vol. 18 No. 1, pp. 42-63

Book and cover design
by Via Media Publishing Company

Edited by Michael A. DeMarco, M.A.

Cover illustration

Feodor Tamarsky, 4th dan Takeda Ryu,
and master painter of martial art subjects.
www.tamarskygallery.com

ISBN-13: 978-1544223339
ISBN-10: 1544223331

www.viamediapublishing.com

contents

iv **Preface**
by Michael DeMarco, M.A.

CHAPTERS

1 **The Martial Arts: Rites of Passage, Dramas of Persuasion**
by Sally Harrison-Pepper, Ph.D.

16 **The Ryuha System:**
Continuity and Change in Japanese Martial Culture
by Nyle C. Monday, M.A.

27 **Shotokan Karate as Non-Discursive Intercultural Exchange**
by Lewis Hershey, Ph.D.

37 **Samurai in School: Ryuha in Traditional Japanese Martial Arts**
by H. Paul Varley, Ph.D.

40 **Ryuha in the Martial and Other Japanese Arts**
by G. Cameron Hurst, III, Ph.D.

54 **Kabala in Motion:**
Kata and Pattern Practice in the Traditional Bugei
by Karl F. Friday, Ph.D.

69 **Ideal Teaching: Japanese Culture and the Training of the Warrior**
by Wayne W. Van Horne, Ph.D.

80 **Modern Educational Theories**
and Traditional Japanese Martial Arts Training Methods
by John Donohue, Ph.D.

107 **Kaho: Cultural Meaning and Educational Method in Kata Training**
by John Donohue, Ph.D.

120 **Progressive Instruction Inherent in Standardized Form Practice**
Using Iaido for Illustration
by Kimberley Taylor, M.Sc.

152 **Index**

preface

In contrast to the overabundance of writings about martial arts that are often promotional and misinformative, there are rare works by scholars that are praiseworthy for their sincere, unbiased approach to writing. This is the very definition of "scholarly." This two-volume anthology brings together the best scholarly works published in the *Journal of Asian Martial Arts* on the topic of teaching and learning Japanese martial arts.

In this volume, you'll find ten chapters that dive deep into Japanese martial traditions, combining aspects of history and culture that explain how teaching methods developed and evolved. Dr. Harrison-Pepper's chapter sets the tone with a focus on the fundamental student–teacher relationship that is responsible for the transmission of any art. She uses sociological and performance studies to analyze the martial art's maturing process.

Understanding the teacher-student relationship is vital for all involved Japanese combative arts. Since Japan was ruled by a warrior class for nearly 700 years, it is necessary to understand the method by which warriors were educated through the *ryuha* system. Nyle Monday's chapter presents this system.

Dr. Lewis Hershey explores the way in which a martial art can serve as a vehicle for non-discursive intercultural exchange in the teaching process. His chapter provides a discussion of the importance of embodying the feeling or aesthetic of a particular system as a way of knowing and understanding martial techniques.

The next three chapters were originally prepared for a meeting of the Association for Asian Studies. Dr. Paul Varley states that most who have written about martial arts practice are not trained scholars and their writings vary greatly in quality. He discusses the state of writing in this field and introduces the other authors.

Dr. Cameron Hurst discusses the characteristics of the martial arts that place them squarely into the category of "artistic ways" along with such familiar arts as Noh, the tea ceremony, and flower arranging. This reflects the "family headship" system of instruction to carry on the school's traditions.

Dr. Karl Friday defines the term *ryuha* as "branch of the current," representing the onward flow of a stream of thought; the branches betoken the splitting off that occurs as insights are passed from master to students, generation after generation. His chapter shows how ryuha exist to hand on knowledge with pattern practice (*kata*) being the core of transmission.

Is it warrior's individualism that is prized in modern conformity-ridden Japanese culture, or is this an erroneous interpretation of the idealized warrior image by Westerners? In the next chapter, Dr. Wayne VanHorne's research is persuading, showing that the ultimate goal of the training is to foster individuals to contribute to the betterment of the collective society with social responsibility.

In the following chapter, Dr. John Donohue analyzes the organizational components of traditional martial arts training and relates them to modern pedagogical theories. He concludes that the instructional theory embedded in martial arts training is at least as sophisticated and highly developed as are the techniques and philosophies of these systems. In the next chapter, he examines kata training as (1) a cultural activity that has been shaped by the structural characteristics of Japanese culture, and kata training as (2) a highly structured and effective mechanism for imparting technical skill in the martial arts.

Kim Taylor provides the final chapter dealing with "progressive instruction" found in many kata-based martial arts. Using *iaido* (sword drawing) as an example, he demonstrates how a set of practice can build—one kata after the other—from simple to more complex ideas and provide a deeper understanding of the entire set.

If you are interested in Japanese martial traditions, you will find much in these ten chapters that clarify why the arts are taught according to a long-standing tradition—and also why there have been evolutionary changes in the instructional methods. There is sound logic for the old traditions, as well as for the changes. The scholarly research presented in this anthology will improve a teacher's way of instructing and help a student understand what to expect out of his or her studies.

Michael A. DeMarco, Publisher
Santa Fe, New Mexico
March 2017

Notes

chapter 1

The Martial Arts:
Rites of Passage, Dramas of Persuasion
by Sally Harrison-Pepper, Ph.D.

Passages can be elaborate gateways often symbolically
decorated according to their political or religious
importance. Other passageways hold importance
as images which are psychologically significant.
Photos by M. DeMarco.

Traditional martial artists believe that the physical disciplines practiced by Shaolin Temple monks during the seventh century formed the matrix for their art. Martial arts instructor Gichin Funakoshi, for example, includes the story of Bodhidharma's journey from western India to China's Henan Province in his book *Karate-Do: My Way of Life* (1975). Arriving at the Shaolin Temple to present lectures on Buddhism, Bodhidharma was so distressed by the physical exhaustion of its monks that he "set forth a method of developing the mind and body, telling them: "Although the way of Buddha is preached for the soul, the body and soul are inseparable. . . . I shall give you a method by which you can develop your physical strength enough to enable yourselves to attain the essence of the way of Buddha" (Funakoshi, 1975: 7). Thus, Funakoshi emphasizes, the Shaolin martial arts were fundamentally connected to their goals of spiritual perfection.

Eugen Herrigel, in *Zen in the Art of Archery*, similarly affirms a link between archery and Zen, pointing out that the very methodicalness of Zen presents a blending of technique, style, and spirit which supports a system of rigorous physical as well as spiritual training.

> There is a practicalness about Zen which inspires confidence. So it is not surprising if, for the same reason that the way has to be divided up, schematically and thematically, into single steps, the learning of these steps should turn into a regular routine. There is a rigorous training in Zen which strikes one as utterly soulless. Everything must go with clockwork precision.
>
> —Herrigel, 1971: 23

Traditional martial arts instructors train the body and mind for a condition of living which extends far beyond the acquisition of the black belt. Indeed, as Funakoshi's book title indicates, the martial arts become a "way of life" for those who have been trained in the traditional, Zen-based system. Some theater practitioners, too, recognize the value of training one's body and mind as a totality. In his 1982 essay on "Theatre Anthropology," for example, Eugenio Barba describes the importance of "extra-daily" techniques, "techniques which do not respect the habitual conditionings of the body," as devices to teach actors about energy, immobility, limits, simplification, and the power of a "decided body" (1982: 9).

"The way we use our bodies in daily life," Barba explains, "is substantially different from the way we use them in performance" (1982: 7). In both Kabuki and Noh, for example, the hips are central to the actor's extra-daily technique. In the working terminology of Kabuki, an actor is said to have *ko-shi*, "hips," when he has the right energy while working. Barba explains:

> When we walk according to daily body techniques, the hips follow the legs. In the extra-daily techniques of the Kabuki actor, and of the Noh actor, the hips, on the contrary, remain fixed. To block the hips while walking it is necessary to slightly bend the knees and, engaging the vertebral column, to use the trunk as a single unit, which then presses downwards. In this way two different tensions are created in the upper and lower parts of the body.
>
> —Barba, 1982: 10

Interestingly, the extra-daily technique of the martial arts is identical: the hips remain fixed as the martial artist moves forward in one of three basic stances. Often, an instructor holds the hips of a *karateka* (karate student). In addition, new students are told to place the uniform belt below the waist and around the hips in order to emphasize this important point of tension and balance.

In an earlier essay on actor training, Barba says that a good program:

> does not teach how to act, how to be clever, does not prepare one for creation. Training is a process of self-definition, a process of self-discipline which manifests itself indissolubly through physical reactions. It is not the exercise in itself that counts—for example, bending or somersaults—but the individual's justification for his own work.... This inner necessity determines the quality of the energy which allows work without a pause, without noticing tiredness, continuing even when exhausted and at that very moment going forward without surrendering. ... Training puts one's own intention to the test.
>
> –Barba, 1972: 47

In traditional martial arts training as well, daily practice puts one to the test. Karate skills are a totality of experience, a part of one's passage toward a more centered, more aware self, so that techniques are closely connected to notions of discipline, precision, and concentration. Through exhaustive, repetitive exercises, the martial artist tackles the persistent and fundamental problems of concentration and relaxation, problems we try to solve in our actor-training programs as well.

Combat exercises further develop one's center through an immersion in oppositions. Balanced between aggression and fear, moving and not-moving, tension and relaxation, students learn to surrender to the demands of a sparring partner, not as adversary, my master used to say, but as a teacher, one who will illuminate one's weaknesses. "It is a contest of the archer with himself," Herrigel remarks (1971: 19). The self, then, becomes the sole obstacle to good sparring and good training, and this is true for much more than the martial arts. Observes theater director and theorist Jerzy Grotowski: "If an actor has the will to express, then he is divided: there is a part of him doing the willing and another part doing the expressing, a part which is commanding and another which carries out the commands" (Barba, 1982: 27).

From 1971 to 1976, I trained with Master Ki Whang Kim, a ninth-degree black-belt and traditional teacher of Moo Duk Kwon T'angsoodo, a Korean style of Taekwondo. I received my first-degree black belt in 1976. From 1976 to 1982, I studied in New York City and received my second-degree in 1981. Between 1980 and 1985, I also trained as a Performance Theorist in New York University's Department of Performance Studies. The years of my combined training produced several moments of deep learning, in which I experienced valuable insights about the nature of training. These insights emerged from my experiences within a system of training explicitly designed to prompt a greater respect for the unity of mind and body. They are, therefore, useful motivational devices for performers as well as martial artists. I've found the following experiences to be the most useful in terms of actor training.

An old picture shows Chen Taijiquan master Du Yuze at the All Asia Gongfu Tournament held in Taipei, Taiwan. Here he is performing Buddha's Guardian Pounds Pestle (*Jin Gang Dao Tui*). Photo is from a booklet published to celebrate Du's eightieth birthday. It was published in Taiwan by his disciple, Mr. Wang Jiaxiang.

On the Threshold

In September, 1971, I enrolled in karate classes at Kim Studio in Rockville, Maryland. I received a uniform and was told to return for classes at 5:45 p.m., at which time I would be instructed in proper studio etiquette. When I returned, I was asked to remove my shoes and place them on a rack beside the door. I was told to bow to the Korean flag at the front of the studio—feet together, hands at the sides, eyes on the flag, bent at the waist (an American flag was there as well, but it was not mentioned during my instruction). I crossed to the dressing room door and repeated the bow. I performed it once again when I returned in uniform. Each doorway, then, was marked by a formal, stylized gesture. Once inside the studio, I approached each black belt and bowed with a verbal greeting: "Good evening, sir" (there were no women black belts at the time).

This physical act became a significant persuasive tool in my development and orientation to the martial arts. Though at first I performed this routine only because I was told to do so, doing so later began to alter my beliefs. This, as Barbara Myerhoff observed, is one of the special tasks of ritual action: to persuade its practitioners that what is occurring is significant, sacred, or set apart in some way. Ritual, Myerhoff says, "is an act or actions intentionally conducted by a group of people employing one or more symbols in a repetitive, formal, precise, highly stylized fashion. Action is indicated because rituals persuade the body first; behaviors precede emotions in the participants" (1977: 199).

The doorway bow, as an act of deliberate demarcation, a frame, came to mark not only my physical passage from one place to another, but also my spiritual passage from one world to another. Indeed, I came to rely on the bow as a trigger, a device which would systematically suspend the world outside the studio through a ritualized sequence of actions. The bow said "I am here" and, at the same time, "I am not there." It was, therefore, a ritual of both separation and inclusion: my mind was persuaded to shift its focus to other concerns, a quest for center, posture, obedience, rules, repetition, strength, endurance (concerns which did not exist, at least not to the same degree, outside the studio), while, as a gesture of surrender and humility, the threshold ritual also enhanced and supported the studio's overall structure of beliefs. The bow announced my presence and my attention.

> Ritual gestures announce instrumental activities very often. As such they call the subject's attention to his undertaking. He is acting with awareness. He has taken the activity out of the ordinary flow of habit and routine, and performed the gesture to arouse in himself a particular attitude, demonstrating that his actions mean more than they seem.
> —Myerhoff, 1977: 200

The bows to the black belts revealed additional information about the specialized order of the studio, an order which rearranged ordinary hierarchies of occupation, economic status, age, gender, or race simply by focusing on a colored cloth belt around a plain white uniform. Each black belt's response became a comment on the karateka's training attitude: a nod indicated "adequacy"; a verbal greeting combined with a short bow implied a sense of mutual respect; no response, indicated that an essential training attitude was lacking, patience or perhaps humility. Both bowing sequences then, in the doorway and to the black belts, framed the activities of the studio as special, unique, or different from those outside the studio.

I've since developed similar threshold rituals within the theater rehearsal hall—the removal of shoes, a code of silence, a greeting—prior to a required warm-up and exercise session. Actors are thereby supplied with an important triggering device which may similarly separate them from previous concerns and include them in the action of the impending rehearsal. As rehearsals proceed, additional greetings expressing relationships to the group may be created: the actor playing a rebellious son may choose to greet his father with a stare; the father-actor may respond with a small shove.

High Courtesy

It was quiet in the karate studio during training. A sharp exhalation of breath, the snap of a uniform or the formal *kiai* (shout) were the only predictable sounds of training. Questions or discussions were infrequent. Students did not "play around" with the prescribed regimen. The atmosphere was disciplined, focused and respectful. Interactions were on the level of "high courtesy," a state in which participants suppress displays of dissatisfaction, boredom, or embarrassment, even satisfaction or joy. "All must collude so as not to spoil the show, or damage the illusion that the dramatic reality coincides with the 'other, out-there reality'" (Myerhoff, 1977: 222).

To a particularly clumsy initiate, this structure was somehow reassuring. The repetition of techniques, in which all ranks pursued a similar goal, was space in which students could learn with a minimum of self-consciousness. Competition was internalized—between parts of the body, between the mind and body—rather than between individuals, and learning was accomplished through observation and repetition. One evening, I realized that squeezing my fists focused my attention. Instructors simply told me to do it; my mind was persuaded through practice rather than explanation. "You go and you do," Master Kim used to say. Certainly it is important to devise ways in which the actors may similarly "go and do" in a focused and respectful environment.

Two early moments of teaching shifted my attitude not only toward training, but also toward my sense of self. Each illustrates the way in which physical training may release self awareness on multiple levels. The following describes these experiences.

"Ki" and Self-Mastery

For much of my life, I was very shy. I rarely went out. I withdrew in social situations. When forced to go to parties, I was the girl sitting in the corner intently studying the wallpaper. In the studio too, I was quiet, restrained, and unassertive. For nearly three months, I didn't kiai during my techniques: I opened my mouth with my classmates, but allowed their noise to obscure my own lack of sound. One evening, instructor Albert Cheeks discovered my deception.

Cheeks told the class to sit down and proceeded to devote nearly twenty minutes to coaxing, threatening, and finally demanding my kiai. I squeaked, I made small strange sounds, I promised to work on it alone, and I generally tried to talk my way out of his demands. Finally, in anger and frustration, I yelled a word that might have terminated my training. Cheeks simply praised its focused energy and suggested I try another word in the future. The class lined up again to train.

This simple incident became a moment of deep learning. I saw, through my response to Cheek's demands, that my "shyness" was motivated by a felt need to suppress aggressiveness: it wasn't "feminine" and, therefore, embarrassed me. But the goals of self-mastery inherent in traditional karate training are designed precisely to reveal and address this conflict. Later, I learned that the Noh concept of "energy" is also expressed as *kiai*, meaning a 'profound agreement' (*ai*) of the spirit (*ki*) with the body. In the martial arts, the kiai is said to erupt from the energy produced by a unity of intention and enactment, spirit and body.

As I achieved greater self-mastery, I found that my kiai offered opportunities to control and redirect the focused energy of combativeness. I overcame the fear that what I was doing wasn't "feminine" and instead focused on becoming the best person I could be. In time, my confidence extended into other areas: I learned to live alone, returned to college, and moved to New York City. I called upon my center, my ki, in times of stress.

Certainly actors also experience conflicts within their training. Things come up as part of one's rehearsal for a role that may surprise or embarrass the performer. "Who is that person?" she wonders. "That's not me!" he insists. Yet actors, directors, and other performance theorists know that confronting the unknown, mysterious being within yields a wealth of material for performance. With practice in non-aggressive, inner-directed confrontation, the performer may learn to redirect himself toward a greater range and depth of preformulated expressions, to encourage rather than restrain the self. "How far is one prepared to pay with one's own person for all that one believes and declares?" Barba asks. "It is the possibility of bridging the gap between intention and realization. This daily task, obstinate, patient, often in darkness, sometimes even searching for a meaning for it, is a concrete factor in the transformation of the actor" (1972: 47).

No, Sir!

At the end of a workout, Master Kim often approached a new student and commented upon the difficulty of the workout. "Oh, you look very tired," he would say. "Are you tired?" Woe to the uninitiated student who answered "Yes." Master Kim would demand fifty push-ups! Kim would then turn to a wiser, though equally tired student and repeat the question, "Are you tired?" "No, Sir!" the student would yell. Kim would tell him or her to sit down and rest.

In Kim's "go and do" training method, karateka were thus encouraged to present positive, energetic attitudes, despite actual pain or fatigue. At first, however, this seemed an unnatural demand for theatrics, an inauthentic or dishonest exchange between student and master. But I did not yet understand that action precedes emotion in the martial arts. One hot summer evening, the sweat dripping off my brow and my breath coming in short, irregular spurts, Master Kim asked me, "Are you tired?" No, Sir!" I shouted. The collusion of fellow students supported my pretense, and suddenly I was no longer tired. Through repetition and observation, the "demonstration" became "actual."

This technique remains useful. For example, I established a rule of behavior in my rehearsals prohibiting the word "tired," as well as any attitudes which might reflect it (lying down, yawning, and so on). As in the karate studio, the result is a reinvigoration of the performers through an action of will which persuades the body that it is not tired.

Kata, Flow, and Performance

The repetitive practice of kata or forms in the martial arts offers additional ideas about training. Kata consist of a series of carefully choreographed movements organized into a set of increasingly difficult exercises. Two or three forms are assigned to each rank, and they have supposedly been transmitted from instructor to instructor over the centuries. It is said that each kata is designed to teach not only increasingly complex movement styles, but also progressively elevated states of mind. Master Kim told me, for example, that one must practice the first white belt form 5,000 times before reaching the black belt. Through daily practice, he explained, the body "knows" what to do, the mind is temporarily suspended, and ki enters form.

Mihalyi Csikszentmihalyi, a University of Chicago behavioral scientist, describes this ideal quality of mind as "flow," a peculiar yet pleasant feeling of total involvement experienced during the performance of certain familiar, practiced activities. In flow, Csikszentmihalyi found, actions seem to proceed logically from one to the next; necessary skills, acquired through training, repetition, and practice, seem to come naturally. Remarked a mountain climber, "It's self-catalyzing...The moves...create each other.... You just do it without reflecting on it at the time" (1976: 86-88). Surgeons said they were "much less aware of self or personal problems," or were "totally enmeshed" in their actions during difficult operations (1974: 211). Chess players were unaware of fatigue, hunger, or anxiety during complex games. In interviews, mountain climbers, surgeons, chess players, rock dancers, and professional athletes all noted that this sensation was so pleasurable that they often devoted inordinate amounts of time or energy to their activities. Had Csikszentmihalyi interviewed performers, he would surely have found comparable descriptions and experiences among them.

In the martial arts too, devoted karateka describe a sense of floating or flowing within their kata. Mike Kennelly described the benefits of repetition in sparring: "Once you have learned and mastered certain formalized modes of interaction, you diminish fear, thus releasing the mind to float with the experience. In fact, repetition of behavior both releases the fear and causes the student to learn with the sense more than the mind, which then has the secondary effect of maximizing performance" (1982: 73). Herrigel, too, seems to describe flow in the following passage: "One only knows and feels that one breathes. And, to detach oneself from this feeling and knowing, no fresh decision is required, for the breathing slows down of its own accord, becomes more and more economical in the use of breath, and finally, slipping by degrees into a blurred monotone, escapes one's attention altogether." Herrigel adds, however, that "this exquisite state of unconcerned immersion in oneself is not, unfortunately, of long duration. It is liable to be disturbed from inside" (1971: 65-57). One of the goals of repetitive training, then, is to reduce the frequency of these inside interruptions.

In contemporary performing arts, one need only examine the work of Robert Wilson, Steve Reich, Meredith Monk, or Philip Glass, to name a few, to see the benefits of repetition in both training and performance. Critic Theodore Shank, for example, says the following about Wilson's performance in theater: "Slow motion over an extended period alters drastically the way we perceive the performance. It tends to carry one beyond boredom, beyond the point of being irritated by the slowness, and one tends to adapt by slipping into a mental state that is less acutely conscious than normal. This state of reduced consciousness makes possible the intended mode of perception" (Shank, 1982: 126).

And Wilson felt that his theatrical structure became more visible with the help of Glass's musical compositions through the cyclic forms in which rhythm and repetition predominate over melody and harmony. Through an additive process, a musical phrase is repeated over and over, then changed slightly and repeated again, and so forth. Through repetition, then, one is able to perceive the process and flow with it.

Dramas of Persuasion

The rituals of martial arts training are fused into a single dramatic occasion, a "socially provided crisis" (Myerhoff, 1977: 220) in which borders are crossed, identity symbols are stripped away, and the person becomes most teachable. The occasion is the examination for a new rank. And while the passage to each rank is significant, the rites of passage connected with the transition to black belt are particularly important.

The ordeal begins when a brown belt successfully performs the techniques, forms, sparring, and board-breaking demonstrations necessary for candidacy at an examination. A black stripe added to the brown belt becomes a formal marker of candidacy, thrusting the unsuspecting karateka into an uncertain and sometimes terrifying "limbo of statuslessness" between student and black belt (Turner, 1969: 97).

In *The Ritual Process* (1969), Victor Turner described the ways in which ritual behavior reclassifies or inverts usual norms of behavior in a three-phase process first outlined by Belgian folklorist Arnold Van Gennep in 1909. Van Gennep calls these phases, (1) separation, (2) margin or limen, and (3) aggregation. In the first phase of a puberty rite, for example, the pre-pubescent boy is physically separated from his tribe in a ritually prescribed place. During the middle phase, the boy's candidacy for manhood is tested in one or more terrifying or painful rites. At the conclusion of his ordeal, he is reintegrated into his tribe as a man. Turner focuses on the middle stage of this rite of passage, a phase he came to call the "liminal," from the Latin *limen* for "threshold."

As a physical space, the limen of a doorway is not usually a space one remains in for long nor a place one notices in the act of crossing (unless it is marked by a threshold ritual). But when the limen becomes the "liminal," a phase one moves through in order to get from one fixed social structure to another, it becomes a place of great potency and potentiality in culture. Ambiguous and paradoxical, it is a time for teaching and decision, play and experiment. When one remains in the liminal for an extended period of time, profound changes may occur.

Richard Schechner demonstrated liminality by standing in the doorway to his New York University classroom. Neither in the classroom nor outside of it, he stood, literally, between two places. Sometimes, he'd move out into the hall and talk to his students from outside. Then, he'd step inside to speak. Finally, he'd return to the doorway, the place of the liminal, and remain there for five, ten, fifteen minutes. Initially, students laughed as their professor stood in a doorway to deliver his lecture. But when the demonstration was prolonged, students grew anxious. They clearly wished that Schechner would return to the room, to the normal social order. His physical demonstration thus was not only playful, but also disturbing. Ultimately, however, the significance of the liminal lies in an understanding of its quality of openness, that it occurs between established cultural systems and sub-systems and, therefore, allows for deeper understanding of one's place in the structure to emerge.

In the martial arts, my liminal status as "black belt candidate" was defined through ambiguous, contradictory behavior, trials and ordeals. I was excluded from the customary treatment of students, while not yet accorded the respect given to black belts. I meditated in neck-high ice water as a test of endurance; I obeyed unusual commands as a test of discipline; black belts unexpectedly challenged me to spar. Yet one of the most important attributes of the liminal entity is surrender: one must submit to the power of the liminal in order to pass through to reincorporation. Initiates, Turner says, must "submit to an authority that is nothing less than the total community," thereby experiencing a "profound immersion in humility" (1969: 102-3).

Suspended between two states of being, I was forced to reconsider the structure of the studio and my place within it. It was a period of "pure potentiality, when everything, as it were, trembles in the balance" (Turner, 1982: 44). Thus, the psychological state of the neophyte is like the process one undergoes in the creative process. In each, a crucial tension is created in the mind. Then, at some point in the journey, the conscious will is abandoned. One yields to the indeterminate in oneself, while maintaining an extreme watchfulness over the shuffling and reshuffling of ideas. This, in essence, is the process of liminality as well, a "periodical reclassification of reality... and man's relationship to society, nature, and culture" (Turner, 1982: 51).

The Inscription

A neophyte in liminality, Turner says, must become a "*tabula rasa,* a blank slate, on which is inscribed the knowledge and wisdom of the group" (1969: 103), and this part of my training occurred in June, 1976, during Kim Studio's annual training camp. Three other candidates and I stood at attention before nearly one-hundred students. Master Kim walked around us, looking, sighing, growling. After what seemed an eternity, Kim said to me: "You very strong. In Siberia I put, no clothes have, no food have—you survive. Strong. Discipline, yes. More patience must have. You remember *innay* [the Korean word for 'patience']."

Thus, I was inscribed with a word which I was to carry with me throughout my training. In 1979, I was hospitalized following some major knee surgery. Distraught over the future of my martial arts training, I called Master Kim. He said: "You remember I tell you innay. Now this training begins. You train hard." Re-inscribed, I worked through a year of physical therapy and returned to Richard Chun's studio. I received my second degree black belt in 1981.

Reintegration

The final phase of my examination and rite of passage was performed before Master Kim, approximately fifteen black belts, and two witnesses for each candidate. The exam included a written test of Korean vocabulary, an essay on the candidate's martial art philosophy, and demonstrations of kata, kicking, punching, blocking, board-breaking, and sparring. As an occasion of public liminality, examinations were the scene and time for the group's deepest values to emerge. For black belt candidates, the exam was, further, a dramatic occasion in which candidates were encouraged to become conscious of themselves in new ways, to "think about how they think" or "feel about how they feel" (Turner, 1977: 7). It was long, difficult, and terrifying.

At its conclusion, when I was told I had passed, a paradoxical inversion in my expectations occurred. As I stood at attention before Master Kim, ready to receive my black belt, he said: "First degree black belt. Now you in doorway. All this time, you just preparing. Get black belt. You stay, student become. You leave, always in doorway."

Transmission of any art requires a student who possesses natural talent and a qualified teacher. Practice, repetition, and dedication allow one to cross new thresholds and attain greater mastery of his chosen art form. This holds true whether we are talking about turning a potter's wheel or performing music, dance, or a martial arts form. *Photos by M. DeMarco.*

Though I had passed through the liminal phase of my candidacy and might have believed my black belt marked the end of my training, Master Kim returned me to the beginning. Only now, he said, was I ready to become a "student." He wrapped and tied my belt around his waist, transmitting his knowledge into it, and then tied it around me.

Martial Arts and Performance

Turner's concept of liminality is an important tool for both karateka and performance theorists. As a means of describing the recurring phenomena of performative behavior, definitions of the liminal offer a vocabulary that can be shared. Certainly the rite of passage I've described shares many aspects of Turner's tribal rituals. Additionally, however, the beliefs I've adopted are useful in performance training.

It seems that theater exaggerates the liminal as part of its primary process. Fundamental to its expressiveness, for example, is the way in which it lies betwixt-and-between illusion and reality, here and there, then and now. Indeed, the work of art may be defined as occurring exclusively in the limen, with the phases of separation and reincorporation occurring before and after the performance.

An elderly man keeping limber by performing a cane form in a park. Onlookers are often amazed by the intensity and focus exhibited by martial art practitioners. *Photo by M. DeMarco.*

Performers, directors, writers—all the makers of performance—are deeply immersed in the liminal, both in the creation and the performance of their art. Perhaps they don't know how to speak of the process, but they know when they are there, in what John Livingston Lowes calls "the surging chaos of the unexpressed" (in Ghiselin, 1952: 14). And a fundamental activity of the liminay creative process involves what Picasso calls a "series of destructions," destroying the known in order to formulate the unknown.

An understanding of group processes and the apparently necessary ambiguity of the rehearsal phase has, more than once, helped some anxious student actors see the group's tensions and doubts for what they are: an essential phase in the rite of passage called the performance. There always seems to be a point in rehearsal process in which our reasons for working and our fondness for or belief in the show, the director, our fellow actors are all called into question. Yet Turner shows us that this phase of self-doubt is an essential aspect of the liminal, adding that liminal phenomena are "the seedbeds of cultural creativity" (1982: 28).

Certain collective rituals may mark an entire group's rite of passage. In public liminal rituals (such as the Mardi Gras or New Year's Eve in Times Square or in events which involve a collective response to natural or man-made disasters such as earthquakes, wars, or famines) feelings of anxiety, experimentation, or playfulness may be evident. These are times of public reflectiveness which "stress the role of collective innovatory behavior, of crowds generating new ways of framing and modelling the social reality which presses on them in their daily lives. Here all is open, plurally, reflexive, the folk acts on the folk and transforms itself through becoming aware of its situation and predicament" (Turner, 1977: 46).

Perhaps greater occasions for discussion between the practitioners of a variety of body training systems could enhance performer training through an enlarged collection of "extra-daily techniques" ("techniques which do not respect the habitual conditionings of the body" [Barba, 1982: 9]). Neglecting to utilize the potential avenues for understanding this kind of information greatly reduces the maximal performance capabilities of our performers. Training which neglects the body and neglects the importance of discipline and surrender does a great disservice to the creative potential of our performers.

REFERENCES

Barba, E. (1972). Words or presence. *The Drama Review* (T53), Vol. 16, No. 1.

Barba, E. (1982). Theatre anthropology. *The Drama Review* (T94), Vol. 26, No. 2.

Chun, R. (1975). *Moo duk kwan.* Burbank, CA: Ohara Publications.

Csikszentmihalyi, M. (1974). *Flow: Studies of enjoyment.* PHs Grant Report, N. R01 HM 22883002.

Csikszentmihalyi, M. (1975). *Beyond boredom and anxiety*. San Francisco: Jossey-Bass Publishers.

Funakoshki, G. (1975). *Karate-do: My way of life*. Tokyo: Kodansha International, Ltd.

Ghiselin, B. (Ed.). (1952). *The creative process*. New York: New American Library.

Herrigel, E. (1971). *Zen in the art of archery*. New York: Vintage.

Jackson, G. (1978). The conveyance of social beliefs and values through aesthetic sport. In Michael A. Salter (Ed.). *Play: Anthropological perspectives*. New York: Leisure Press.

Kennelly, M. (January, 1982). Imagery and visualization. *Black Belt*, Vol. 20, No. 1.

Myerhoff, B. (1977). We don't wrap red herring in a printed page. In Sally Moore and Barbara Myerhoff (Eds.). *Secular ritual*. Amsterdam: Van Gorcum.

Schechner, R. (1982). *The end of humanism*. New York: Performing Arts Journal Publications.

Shank, T. (1982). *American alternative theatre*. New York: Grove Press.

Turner, V. (1969). *The ritual process*. New York: Cornell Paperbacks.

Turner, V. (1977). Limimality and the performative genres. A paper prepared in advance for participants in *Burg Wartenstein Symposium No. 76*. New York: Wenner-Gren Foundation for Anthropological Research, Aug. 27. Sept. 5.

Turner, V. (1982). *From ritual to theatre: The human seriousness of play*. New York: Performing Arts Journal Publications.

chapter 2

THE RYUHA SYSTEM: CONTINUITY AND CHANGE IN JAPANESE MARTIAL CULTURE
by Nyle C. Monday, M.A.

At Meiji Shrine in January 1977. Left: Donn F. Draeger demonstrates Isshin-ryu Kusarigama-jutsu, a portion of the curriculum of the Shindo Muso-ryu. Right: A portion of the curriculum of the Shinto-ryu Ken-jutsu. *Photos courtesy of N. Monday.*

In recent years there has been a tremendous surge of interest worldwide in the combative methods of Asia, particularly in regards to Chinese *quanfa* (so-called *gongfu*) and in Japanese karatedo. Although this interest has resulted in a steady flow of technical information, the amount of reliable historical and philosophical information accompanying this importation process has been microscopic. We have, in effect, plucked an aspect of a culture out of its cultural "nest" and set it down in a foreign cultural setting minus its values, most of its philosophical trappings and the support system which nurtured it through centuries of development. It is little wonder that there is an appalling lack of understanding as to what, in fact, is a "martial art," what are its attributes and purposes, and how it is to be taught and studied.

The importance of understanding these aspects of "martial arts," particularly in the case of Japan, can hardly be overemphasized. Japan was ruled by the warrior class for nearly seven hundred years. If one wishes to understand Japanese history, it is necessary to understand the warrior and the method by which he was educated. Because the primary function of the warrior was to provide security through combative effectiveness, it would seem obvious that this portion of his training cannot be ignored. This chapter will deal with the vehicle through which comprehensive martial knowledge was imparted to the warrior: the ryuha system.

Before embarking on this study it will be necessary to define some of the terminology. Because there are few similarities between the feudal societies of Europe and Japan, the original Japanese terms will be used in the course of this article. There are two basic categories of martial activity: the *bugei* (of *bujutsu*) and the *budo*. The former can most accurately be translated into English as "martial arts," and the latter as "martial way." Although almost no distinction is made between these two in the West, they differ greatly in purpose, nature and technique.

The bugei are the true martial arts. The names of most bugei are easily recognizable as they contain the suffix *-jutsu* applied after a root word which describes one of the following:

1) the weapon used, e.g., *ken-jutsu* ("sword art")
2) the agent of means, e.g., *ba-jutsu* ("horse art")
3) the action or effect, e.g., *nin-jutsu* ("stealth art")
4) the principle used, e.g., *ju-jutsu* ("yielding art")

The bugei were systematically developed from the tenth century onward by the warrior class as actual battlefield-oriented combative methods. Through these systems the warriors (*bushi*) hoped to cultivate the technical skills and frame of mind which would insure their survival and the collective security of their clans. Because of these requirements, the bugei had to be vigorous, practical arts. Moreover, the bushi had to be prepared both to use and face a wide variety of weapons, so a wide spectrum of arts were practiced.

The bugei classification contains both classical (*ko bu-jutsu*) and modern cognate (*shin bu-jutsu*) art forms. A classical bugei has been defined as an art which has "a tradition established prior to the twentieth century" (Draeger and Smith, 1969: 91). Modern cognate forms are those which have appeared since that time. Karate-jutsu, which was not imported into Japan until shortly after the turn of this century from Okinawa, is a prime example of an art contained in this latter group.

One factor rarely understood by non-practitioners is that not all of the bugei deal directly with the use of weapons. Many were concerned with other aspects of military necessity such as the construction of fortification (*chikujo-jutsu*) or the use of signal fires (*noroshi-jutsu*).

Today, many of the bugei are dying out due to lack of interest. Many old traditions have already passed into oblivion for the lack of young, dedicated students. The demands of such training are so great that few are willing to make the sacrifices which it requires. In an effort to survive, some of the old bugei have converted into budo forms to make themselves more applicable to the needs of modern society. The origin of all budo forms lies in such a transition. Not all bugei have a corresponding budo form, but all budo have a corresponding bugei from which they evolved.

The budo can be immediately recognized by the suffix -*do* contained in their names. The character for *do* is variously translated as "Way" (as in "way of life") or "path." This same character, when read in Chinese, is *dao*, as in Daoism. This "Way" is a spiritual path, which gives some indication of how the budo differ from the bugei.

These forms are generally twentieth century developments stemming from concepts which first appeared in the mid-eighteenth century. The man usually believed to have started this trend was Nakanishi Chuta who, around 1750, developed the *shinai* (a dummy bamboo sword used in modern kendo) and body armor so that students of fencing could practice their technique without doing bodily harm to their opponent (Warner and Sasamori, 1964: 51).

Training in the budo does not always follow the traditional form used by the bugei. The principle of the form is usually stressed over the result of the technique. For this reason the budo have lost part, if not most, of their combative utility. This is acceptable, however, because the goal of the budo is not combat preparedness, but self-perfection of the individual through discipline. Similarly, no true budo can be categorized as a sport. The term "sport" implies an effort to win or to establish a better record. A true budo places no emphasis on competition against an external opponent. This reveals how far sport judo and karatedo have degenerated in this country as well as in Japan. It is questionable whether these martial forms can still be considered genuine budo. As is the case with the bugei, there are both classical (*ko budo*) and modern cognate (*shin budo*) varieties which are defined in the same manner.

With this basic linguistic clarification, it is now possible to begin an examination of the ancient martial traditions (*koryu*) Japan.

The basic organization responsible for the martial education of the warrior class is the *ryu*. In the United States today this word is generally defined as "style" or "school," but these interpretations fall short of the full implications of the Japanese term. For the purpose of this paper, the preferred definition of the late Donn F. Draeger, "tradition," will be used.

The attack of swordsman Kobayashi Ichiro is thwarted through the use of Ikkaku-ryu Jutte-jutsu. A Shinto priest, seen in the upper left corner of the picture, serves as the official witness to this dedicatory display of Shindo Muso-ryu teachings. *Photo courtesy of N. Monday.*

The implications of "style" are too general to equate with the concept of ryu, and the Western notion of "school" tends to imply a stationary institution of learning. If this latter term was extended to "school of thought," it perhaps comes nearer to the mark. It is also important to keep in mind that, while this discussion is centered on martial activities, the Japanese utilize this same system for all classical art forms, from the tea ceremony to flower arranging. Although the focus may change, the mechanism is for the most part the same.

A *ryu*, according to Draeger, is "a corporate body, perpetuated by a line of collateral (*sei*) or non-consanguineous (*dai*) headmasters" (Draeger, 1973a: 21). Although this outlines the basic structure of the ryu, it gives no indication of the nature of the institution. The ryu is a living, active entity with an existence of its own. It is guided in its course by a headmaster and one or more master teachers (*shihan*). The founding of any classical ryu (*koryu*), that is, one established prior to the twentieth century, has always been attributed to some type of divine intervention (*tenshin sho*) which guided the ryu's founder (*shosei*) to new martial principles or techniques. This religious inspiration is commemorated and celebrated in many ways throughout the life of the ryu. For instance, the formal name of a ryu may contain a reference to the particular deity which inspired the founder or to the manner in which this inspiration occurred. For example, Muso Gonnosuke Katsuyoshi, a well-known sixteenth century martial artist, secluded himself on Mount Homan after being defeated by the great Miyamoto Musashi. In the course of his physical and spiritual training, he received divine inspiration through a dream in which he was warned to "be aware of the vitals with a log." This cryptic message led him to design the *jo*, a four-foot-long staff of white oak, and to found the Shindo Muso-ryu (lit. "divine-way dream").

Each ryu is also usually associated with a particular shrine, and yearly dedicatory demonstrations (*hono embu*) are given by ryu members at that shrine as an offering. It is important to note that the vast majority of koryu are affiliated with Shintoism, the native animistic religion of Japan, rather than with Buddhism. The ryu which came under the influence of Zen sects of Buddhism were later historical developments, arising after the era of the classical warrior. Even today it is rare indeed to find a training hall (*dojo*) without a small Shinto shrine in a place of honor.

It must be emphasized that this religious tie pervades all aspects of the ryu. There is an intentional aura of mysticism which surrounds each tradition. Again, this is in part due to the flash of divine inspiration which initially led to the ryu's founding, but it is also a reminder that the ryu and all its members remain under the guidance and protection of the *kami* (gods). This link between martial arts and religion is often dismissed by foreign observers as just another example of "Oriental mysticism," but it fulfills a specific and essential need within the framework of the ryu, and through these practices the scope of the ryu's teachings takes on an entirely new dimension. The purpose of the ryu, after all, is to promote individual and group security. Religion is only an extension of this aim, for what is religion other than the ultimate form of self-defense?

In addition to its affiliation with a shrine, ryu are quite often also associated with a particular martial family or clan. The classical martial arts, as taught by a headmaster, were the ultimate weapons of that age, and the clans who held (or hoped to hold) power did their best to attract the finest teacher available. The ability to do this would, to a great extent, determine the strength of their warriors. As a result, most of the classical ryu have a political affiliation of this sort. The Tenshin Shoden Katori Shinto-ryu, one of the few classical ryu widely known outside of Japan, is a rare exception to this rule. In fact, this particular koryu has had exponents among both the Genji (Minamoto) and Heike (Taira), the two most powerful martial clans, whose rivalry is chronicled over several hundred years of Japanese history. The Yagyu Shinkage-ryu, on the other hand, has been associated with the Tokugawa family ever since Yagyu Tajima-no-kami Munenori was appointed as fencing master to Shogun Tokugawa Ieyasu in 1594.

Gaining admission to a ryu was (and still is) not simply a matter of applying; entry was strictly controlled. A person of non-warrior class had no chance of being accepted. During the Tokugawa era (1603-1868), the warrior class declined to such an extent that non-warriors were permitted to establish and participate in their own combative disciplines derived from superficial aspects of the true warrior martial arts. These disciplines are usually termed "martial arts" in the West today even though they are usually *budo* ("martial ways") as opposed to *bugei/bu-jutsu* ("martial arts"), and they are most often of a civilian origin. It might thus be far more accurate to term them "civil ways" rather than "martial arts." Even today, aspirants to koryu membership are often required to have the proper background as well as a recommendation from someone of importance within the ryu. Even the handful of foreigners who have gained entrance in the past few decades have not been exempt from this selection process. Most have either police or military background, the nearest Western equivalent to being of the warrior class.

Upon being accepted into a ryu, the student undergoes an initiation, usually including the taking of a blood oath (*kappan*). Because of the necessity of keeping the ryu teachings secret, the trainee is sworn to silence under the threat of divine retribution. The mystique of the ryu, after all, is a potential weapon itself. Consider, for example, a duel (*shinken shobu*) between two swordsmen of different ryu. Before beginning such a combat, it was not unusual to exchange introductions, often including one's ryu affiliation.

In some cases this was not done until after the combat to avoid embarrassing one's teacher and the ryu in the event of defeat. Even if no such announcement was made (and the reputation of the opposing swordsman had not preceded him), the ryu of a particular swordsman could sometimes be identified by distinctive techniques (*waza*) or combative postures (*kamae*).

Many ryu were famous for a particular secret technique. Often the names of the waza were legendary even among the common folk although the actual mechanics were unknown. A good example of this is the famous *tsubame gaeshi* ("swallow turn") of Sasaki Kojiro. The name of this technique is widely known even today among Japanese, but only a very few select members of koryu know how to actually perform it. The psychological effect of facing a swordsman, knowing that he possesses a deadly unknown technique, can hardly be underrated. In a life-or-death situation, even a moment of fear or hesitation will lead to defeat. There was only one way to overcome this: training.

The basis of all martial training within these traditions is kata. Kata are prearranged series of techniques performed either solo or, more usually, between to cooperating partners. These forms are, in effect, an encyclopedia of the ryu's techniques united into a combatively realistic sequence. This type of training typifies the classical ryu. Any so-called "martial art" which advocated free-style, non-prearranged sparring (other than actual combat) is not a true bugei. For example, it would be impossible to engage in a free-style fencing match without modifying the weapon and the technique and/or devising protective equipment of some variety to prevent injury. These modifications change the very nature of the art into something not unlike a sport. There must be a referee, points are scored, etc. Moreover, many potentially lethal techniques must be eliminated even though extensive safety precautions have been taken. What is left after this transformation bears little resemblance to the original art. Another less obvious change has also taken place. The inherent danger of the training develops in the student that state of mind necessary to ensure survival on the battlefield. The koryu student has been trained with real weapons, real opponents, and often on outdoor terrain. His training has literally been "under the sword," and he has thereby been able to develop *zanshin*, which Draeger translated as "alertness remaining form":

> This term signifies physical form united with mental acuity and concentration, resulting in uninterrupted dominance over an adversary. There could be no effective fighting skill without it. Zanshin was the undeniable mark of an expert technician; it could not be faked. It was the result of countless hours of experience in combative training and was expressed through physical posture. Through zanshin the bushi achieved the proper mental and physical attitude with which to dominate his adversary.   –Draeger, 1973a: 21

It is important to note that training within a ryu was not limited to the use of a single weapon. The ryu taught a balanced curriculum, well suited to creating an efficient warrior. A wide spectrum of martial arts were taught, ranging from swordsmanship (*ken-jutsu*) to using signal fires (*noroshi-jutsu*) and building fortifications (*chikujo-jutsu*). Each ryu has its own specialty, but it never neglected to give its members experience in using (and facing) as many types of weapons as possible. On occasion, the specialty arts of another ryu might be incorporated into the ryu curriculum, as is the case in the Shindo Musu-ryu.

The ryu has been a tightly integrated, "living" body, not unlike an extended family. The Confucian concepts of interpersonal relations find their expression in the ryu through such relationships as teacher/disciple (*sensei/deshi*), senior student/junior student (*sempai/kohai*), and headmaster/headmaster. This last concept indicates the duty each generation of headmaster owes to his predecessors and to those who will carry on after he himself is gone.

The fate of the ryu is in his hands and he is under obligation to see that it not only survives, but flourishes while he is responsible for it; the continuity of the ryu must be preserved. This, in turn, explains the conservative nature of the ryu, but it should not be misinterpreted to mean that there is no room for innovation. Not only are new ideas accepted, they are expected. However, changes are not taken lightly. Because the teachings of the ryu are designed to provide collective security, any changes must enhance that intention. These arts were perfected on the battlefield. They work, or else their exponents would not have survived to pass them on. Innovations must prove their worth in a similar manner before they may be integrated into the ryu's curriculum.

Within the koryu, exponents are ranked according to the menkyo system. This is a series of from three to seven certificates or licenses which are awarded for varying levels of proficiency. The well known *dan-kyu* system, in which a series of colored belts denote rank, was not developed until 1882 and so was never used in traditional ryu. There was no such thing as a "black belt" swordsman. Generally, no insignia of any sort was worn, so there was no visible indication of an exponent's level of skill.

The study of the bugei was a life-long pursuit, usually begun at a relatively young age. All males of the warrior class were required to undergo this rigorous training, and women received instruction to a lesser extent as well. It is interesting to note that the inner precincts of palaces and family mansions were often guarded by women of the household, who were most commonly armed with a lighter version of the warrior's *naginata* (a type of halberd).

Upon reaching a certain level of expertise, the practitioner was encouraged to undertake the study of one or more other ryu. Often ryu whose headmasters were on friendly terms would take in each other's students at this point in their training, but this was not always the case. The object of this practice was to give the student wider experience in martial arts and to expose him to other methods and ideas.

After this period of cross-training, or sometimes as a means of achieving it, the swordsman would often embark on what has been termed a "wandering martial apprenticeship" (*musha shugyo*) (Dann, 1978: 239). It is this period of training that is often depicted in popular literature in tales of "wandering swordsmen." The method of *musha shugyo* varied. It usually took one of three basic forms: simply visiting various dojo and asking to be allowed to train there; *dojo arashi* (dojo "storming"), that is, walking into a dojo and challenging the headmaster to a duel; or tracking down and duelling with swordsmen of note, not unlike the American gunman's quest to be the "fastest gun in the West." The second of these methods, *dojo arashi*, was particularly interesting. A headmaster could not refuse to duel with an interloper without losing face. Generally, this meant he had to fight this swordsman of unknown ability, but usually not before testing him against some of his senior students. The only alternative was to quietly bribe the newcomer to persuade him to withdraw. To face such a person and lose meant either death or, at least, the loss of one's reputation and livelihood. The seriousness of these encounters cannot be overemphasized. Duels were fought with either practice swords made of oak or with live blades. Death or serious injury was commonplace.

If the swordsman was very successful in making a name for himself, he might choose to part from his teacher and either set up a branch of his old ryu or establish a totally new ryu of his own. A branch ryu was termed a *ha*. For example, Ono Jirouemon Tadaaki was a student of Ito Ittosai Kagehisa, the founder of Itto-ryu. When Ono left his teacher, he formed the Ono-ha Itto-ryu. This sort of martial tradition follows the same general teachings as its forerunner but with minor modifications. The founding of a totally new ryu was probably the most common occurrence. Over seven thousand martial ryu have so far been catalogued by scholars.

The progression of a student through this educational process is explained by the Japanese through the concept of *shu-ha-ri*:

> *Shu-ha-ri* is, in fact, an equation. It describes the stages of development which all exponents may attain if they will but acquire sufficient experience in martial disciplines. It is an irreversible equation. When the order of this equation is ignored, or when the equation itself is unknown, those persons so involved cannot truly be said to have even a conceptual understanding of the classical martial disciplines. So important is it for any exponent of martial disciplines to understand *shu-ha-ri* that failure to do so will unavoidably bring him misunderstandings about these disciplines. —Kuroda, 1974a: 52-53

Shu (literally "defend" or "protect"), the first stage, denotes an exponent's dedication to study and train within a specific martial ryu. This period is given to building a technical foundation upon which all future learning will be based and encompasses the student's passage from a novice to an expert within a single ryu. There is no standard time period for this stage; it is up to the headmaster to indicate when this phase is complete. *Ha* (literally "to break") implies that the exponent "possesses expert skill in the techniques of his original ryu and is liberated from the highly intense kind of concentration of his energies such as was necessary in learning those skills" (Kuroda, 1974b: 52-53). The swordsman now responds to threats automatically, without the need for conscious thought. In this stage he is allowed to begin the study of other ryu but must never fail to maintain the skills of his original tradition. *Musha shugyo* is also often undertaken at this stage of training as well. The final stage, *ri* (literally "to separate"), indicates the natural desire of the expert practitioner to create a martial tradition of his own. By this time he is an accomplished expert in the teachings of several ryu. He is now allowed to sever his ties with his original ryu without criticism to devote himself to the organizing of his new tradition. The *ri* stage is also expressed in the exponent who succeeds to the position of headmaster of his original ryu. Although he has not created a new ryu of his own, he has the responsibility of preserving the tradition he has inherited as well as adding new innovations.

Shu-ha-ri is thus an expression not only of the cycle of training of the individual but also of the life-cycle of the ryu. The exponent naturally progresses from dependence to independence. Even within the sometimes rigid structure of the Japanese society, the ryuha system gives the practitioner the opportunity to express individuality while still remaining within the confines of tradition.

The ryu, as has been briefly detailed in this chapter, is a successful mechanism for cultural continuity. Although this discussion has dealt strictly with martial traditions, the concept of the ryu is used in virtually all other arts as well, including such diverse activities as flower arranging (*ikebana*) and the tea ceremony (*chanoyu*). As the primary educational apparatus of literally all Japanese art forms, it is quite remarkable that so little scholarly attention has been paid to this little understood system.

More than forty years have passed since the occupation of Japan fostered the widespread flow of Japanese martial activity into the United States and the rest of the Western world. America's traditional Eurocentric thinking, manifested in a scant attention paid to Asia in the education of our citizens, encouraged people to either denigrate the cultures of that region as inferior or to gloss over them as being "quaint." Three Asia-based wars later, we can no longer justify this attitude. Even within the "martial arts" world, many teachers know little or nothing about the cultures from which their arts sprang. There are those, too, who take advantage of this situation by proclaiming themselves *shihan* or *soke* of this-or-that ryu. The time has come for martial practitioners to take responsibility for their disciplines by questioning claims, seeking confirmation and rejecting the fantasies sold to them by the unscrupulous. Part of each individual training should also be to gain a historical and cultural knowledge of their art along with its mechanics. Understanding of the structure and purpose of the *ryuha* system is, therefore, a vital foundation for any student of Japanese combative methods.

REFERENCES

Dann, J. (1978). Kendo in Japanese martial culture: Swordsmanship as self-cultivation. Doctoral dissertation. University of Washington.

Draeger, D. (1973a). *The martial arts and ways of Japan: Vol. 1, Classical bujutsu*. New York: Weatherhill.

Draeger, D. (1973b). *The martial arts and ways of Japan: Vol. 2, Classical budo*. New York: Weatherhill.

Draeger, D. (1974). *The martial arts and ways of Japan: Vol. 3, Modern bujutsu and budo*. New York: Weatherhill.

Draeger, D., and Smith, R. (1969). *Asian fighting arts*. Tokyo: Kodansha International.

Kuroda, I. (1974, January-February). Shu-ha-ri: Part 1. *Martial Arts International*, 1:1, 52-53.

Kuroda, 1. (1974, March-April). Shu-ha-ri: Part 2. *Martial Arts International*, 1:2, 52-53.

Matsui, K. (1993). *The history of Shindo Musu Ryu jojutsu*. Kamuela, HI: International Hoplological Society.

Otake, R. (1977). *The deity and the sword: Katori Shinto ryu, Vol. 1*. Tokyo: Minato Publishing.

Otake, R. (1978). *The deity and the sword: Katori Shinto ryu, Vol. 2*. Tokyo: Minato Publishing.

Otake, R. (1978). *The deity and the sword: Katori Shinto ryu, Vol. 3*. Tokyo: Minato Publishing.

Preston, T. (1965). Some aspects of the Japanese martial arts. Masters thesis.

Shimizu, T. (1976). *Shindo Musu ryu jodo kyohan*. Tokyo: Japan Publications.

Warner, G., and Draeger, D. (1982). *Japanese swordsmanship*. New York: Weatherhill.

Warner, G., and Sasamori, J. (1964). *This is kendo*. Tokyo: Charles E. Tuttle.

chapter 3

SHOTOKAN KARATE AS NON-DISCURSIVE INTERCULTURAL EXCHANGE

by Lewis Hershey, Ph.D.

Middle: The intercultural exchange of information is most prominent when instructor and student are of different nationalities. Here Sensei Tanaka prepares to demonstrate a technique to a mixed class of Asian and Anglo students. *Photo courtesy of Andy Timan, Sandan, South Atlantic Karate Association.* Left: In practicing kata, the Western karateka incorporates non-discursive Asian knowledge and culture. Right: For the Western practitioner, karate must embody the values and understanding on the host Japanese culture. *Photos courtesy of L. Hershey, AAKF-JKA.*

Introduction

This chapter explores the way in which Shotokan karate can serve as a vehicle for non-discursive intercultural exchange. The chapter adopts the perspective of a cultural ethnographer interested in identifying culture-specific knowledge and the process by which that knowledge is transmitted to others. For practitioners of karate, and other martial arts, the article provides a discussion of the importance of embodying the feeling or aesthetic of a particular system as a way of knowing and understanding martial techniques.

Non-Discursive Intercultural Exchange

For most Westerners, martial arts are misunderstood as a form of Asian sports. Steeped in metaphors of competition and game from early childhood, the Western mind typically thinks of martial arts as a kind of Asian version of such fighting sports as boxing or wrestling. Further, some practitioners of martial arts encourage this misinterpretation. For some, it is a small price to pay for recognition and credibility in Western culture: sports heroes are

worshipped, whereas artists in general are held in suspicion. For others, this misconception is accepted at face value; martial arts is simply another form of athletic competition.

Yet, for most serious practitioners of Asian martial arts, the appeal of their particular discipline and study extends far beyond athletics. While it is true that the martial arts can provide superb physical conditioning, few who continue to train year after year do so for that purpose. Rather, they are responding to something more sublime, more intangible, and ultimately, more sustaining to the human spirit than merely the ability to fight well or stay in good physical shape.

This chapter explores the idea that at least some portion of what attracts Westerners to the study of Asian martial arts is the opportunity to participate in a form of intercultural exchange. Central to this thesis is the assumption that intercultural exchange exists on many levels. For example, Hershey (1989) develops the idea that the rituals of Shotokan karate can generate cultural identity through a kind of narrative structure. This structure synthesizes the Western bias for narration as an organizing principle (Fisher, 1984; Myherhoff, 1978) with Sandor's (1986) observation that many cultures perceive words as real actions, creating in their use a new and even physical reality. In this way, the act of practicing karate links the discourse-based Westerner with the action-oriented Asian in the generation of a shared cultural identity. In turn, each participant glimpses something of the other culture in Shotokan ritual, which provides a means for intercultural communication.

Similarly, the practice of martial arts also embodies non-discursive cultural information. While this will seem patently obvious to even the most casual observer, it poses some difficult questions of epistemology for the ethnographer. For while it is true that physical movement in all cultures communicates cultural meaning, it is also the case that the perception of that meaning is biased by the cultural legacy of the receiver. For Westerners,

the participation in Asian martial arts exposes the practitioner to cultural information outside his or her own culture. However, the interpretation of that information can be obfuscated by the biases of Westerners to create meanings based upon discursive experience unique to the technology of writing as it has developed in the West. The epistemological dilemma is also a logistical one: How can the Western ethnographer escape the ever-present biases of language to study, understand, or even appreciate the non-discursive elements of another culture?

> "... karateka hear what their sensei is saying but understand him or her only after accomplishing the technique."

The rest of this chapter explores the bases for discourse-bias in the understanding of cultural identity in the West and the way in which one style of martial arts, Shotokan karate, affords Western practitioners access to non-discursive cultural information that may be absorbed, if not articulated, by the Occidental karateka.

According to Walter Ong (1982), the advent of writing and the technology of printing changed forever how literate cultures experience and interpret the phenomenal world. For Ong, literacy removes the individual from direct phenomenal experience, creating a symbolic world of experience that stands irrevocably between the individual and the assimilation of non-evaluative understanding. Because of the nature of literacy, this powerful technological innovation allows people and cultures to acquire enormous advantages in terms of adaptive information retention and communication of it relative to understand the means for cultural information transmission available to non-literate cultures. However, is also true under Ong's ontology that the literate mind has lost the ability to engage the world without discursive mediation. For in creating the technology of the written word, Western culture at least has imposed a symbolic order of syntax and semantics on the retention of all cultural knowledge. It is not simply the case that we think in language; we only after think in terms of the written word. As Ong notes, the written word is strictly an abstraction—it does not parallel or represent some real-world, physical accomplishing thing. The meaning or symbolization of the physical world provides an incredible economy to the literate mind. We can shape and rearrange ideas much like we have learned to do with mathematical relationships in geometric or algebraic proofs. And, of course, this is no small technological development. The transition from pre-literate to post-literate culture has taken thousands of years. Even the ancient written history of the West, from the Old Testament and the Greek historians and philosophers, preserves much of the way of thinking and feeling that characterizes that transition. But the new technology is not without its price. For while we have gained some advantages in becoming literate, the physical existence of meaning that is an inherent part of the bodily act of speaking has been lost. The ascendance of literacy parallels the rise of rationalism as the desired epistemology of learning.

We seldom "speak" now of what words feel like, what about meaning there is that is embodied, consumed, or made a part of our physical existence (although we often use these kinds of expressions to communicate that we sometimes think of understanding as having more than simply a cognitive dimension!). Rather, even our emotional selves become trapped in the rational literacy of the discursive symbol. In "telling" each other how we feel, we subordinate the legitimacy of emotion to the expression and sharing of cognitively ordered rules of syntax and grammar.

The reader can demonstrate for himself the pervasive nature of literate technology even as he reads this chapter. Try appreciating any aspect of karate by picturing in your mind some movement. Now, explain what it means. No matter how you do it, the communication of the image in the mind is bounded by the subtle biases and limitations of our language. You cannot comprehend anything without the technology of literacy because the symbolic nature of language catches you in a tautological loop of cause and effect, a sort of Catch-22 in which what you know and how you know it are inseparable. Once inside the symbol system of literacy, you cannot distinguish or separate the event of karate from the interpretation of it. The key shortcoming of this phenomenon for Westerners is that they interpret karate in a language other than Japanese. Because karate embodies ideas and meanings that are Japanese, the finer points of understanding can be lost as we interpret our experience in terms of our own language, be it English, French, or German.

If language were the only symbolic form of expression available to human cultures, we might have to resign ourselves to the inevitability of difference and misunderstanding. But you may already be protesting at this point a key aspect of the study of karate: there is more to it than what we in the West refer to as understanding. Even on the symbolic level, there is the assimilation and communication of culturally important experience that is not defined by discourse-based technologies. In short, much of the "meaning" of karate—and of membership in the host Japanese culture by extension—exists in the non-discursive symbolic form of the *kata* (the prearranged forms of simulated combat), *kihon* (basic movements and exercises of blocks, kicks, and punches), and to a lesser extent, *kumite* (sparring). In Shotokan, the style I am most familiar with, this non-discursive experience creates the ties that bind practitioners together across geographical, historical, and cultural discontinuities to create a sense of shared meaning. To explicate how we can benefit from this epistemology of non-discursive symbolism it is useful to draw on the work of Susanne Langer.

Langer is probably the best known student of Ernst Cassirer, the German philosopher of language and symbolism. Langer, who studied with him in this country, built upon his work to examine the relationship between discourse-based symbolism and non-discursive symbolism in art. Her initial book, *Philosophy in a New Key*, separated the study of symbolism into reason, ritual, and artistic expression. Later, in *Feeling and Form*, Langer expanded her study of non-discursive symbolic expression.

For Asian karateka, taking the study of martial arts abroad places the intercultural exchange of information in the forefront. *Photo courtesy of Andy Timan, Sandan, South Atlantic Karate Association, ISKF-JKA.*

Among her many insights into the nature of non-discursive symbolism, Langer offers the student of karate much in her discussion of virtual powers (Langer, 1953: 169-187). For example, Langer notes that the difficulty in critiquing dance as an art form lies in the fact that the language of criticism is one form of symbolic expression and dance is a different, even competing, form of symbolism. As such, the critic is constantly attempting to describe and evaluate one symbol system, literally, in terms that it is not. For Langer, symbolic forms do not translate well into other symbolic forms. Hence, when reading a review of a ballet or other dance, the reader will always be at something of a loss in understanding the review. Langer's advice is to experience, to feel the experience of dance as either a dancer or a virtual participant, but not as a critic. Indeed, it is the ability to elicit virtual participation among receivers that for Langer partially defines symbolic forms. Whether through words, movement, or music, symbolic forms communicate feelings and reactions to experience.

This last point is a little tricky for all of us raised to think of our literate selves as sophisticated and somehow superior to non-literates. This is, of course, an evaluation, for the technology of literacy is only valuable in the sense that its products provide a culture with more adaptive outcomes. Whether or not literacy and discursiveness are "better" than other symbolic forms for the maintenance and adaptation of a culture depends very much upon where you stand. To the materialistic American yuppie, this technology is great. It leads to cars, homes, entertainments, and the accumulation of wealth. To the non-literate inhabitant of an Amazon rain forest, that same technology leads to destruction of the living soul of the forest that sustains all life and leaves human beings preoccupied with competition for strangely inanimate things of no intrinsic value while the world dies. The wonder from the non-literates' point of view is how such an uncivilized people could have ever become so powerful.

What Langer's work reminds us is that language is but one of many forms of symbolic activity and cultural expression. Ong separates language further in terms of the technology of the written versus the spoken word. Anthropologists can find useful guidance from both philosophers, for their works help point the way to identify where non-discursive cultural meanings may be found in culturally-specific actions. The key is to try to recognize the point at which the ethnographer reacts to the non-discursive symbolism that communicates cultural meaning.

For most Westerners, these reactions are immediately translated into words. We constantly describe what we are feeling, to others and to ourselves. And, of course, this pulls us into the tautological circle of literacy. For the study of karate, we must learn to appreciate the meaning, the feeling, of its movement in much the same way that Langer advocates we experience dance.

Of course, karateka already know this, at least intuitively. The opening of each class with *kihon* (basic karate techniques) and the repetition drills of techniques constantly grounds the participant in the experience, the feeling, of karate. To be sure, we attempt to describe in language, for example, how to root a stance correctly, but we also demonstrate, repeat, and embody the technique. It is in this physical experience of karate that the opportunity for non-discursive intercultural exchange exists.

In an earlier paper, I detail how Shotokan ritual creates both narrative cultural identity and a unique, non-Western definition of place for Shotokan practitioners. While I still believe that this is true, I do not suggest that narrative and ritual exhaust the cultural knowledge embedded in karate or even best represent the totality of that experience. Doing karate forces the practitioner to assimilate not only the physics of the movement, but also the unique ways of knowing, of feeling, that are necessarily value statements about feeling and knowing derived from the culture in which Shotokan was formed. As many scholars of the martial arts know, Gichen Funakoshi came from Okinawa to Japan in the 1920's and developed the system we know as Shotokan. As an ethnic Japanese, he records in his system elements of his ethnic group. The movements, experience and feeling in the practice of Shotokan by karateka of all nationalities communicate cultural knowledge, experience, and to some extent, an awareness of the world unique to Japanese culture. Further, the feeling of Shotokan in the moment of participation is a symbolism that cannot be translated into the symbolism of language. Hence, the experience of all karateka and perhaps all martial artists and ethnographers alike: there is more to understanding culture than can be communicated through language.

It remains ironic that we must continue to use language to describe nonlinguistic cultural meaning. Perhaps of some use here are some terms for discussing literary art and poetry. Poetry, like dance or karate, is a symbolic form that attempts to communicate feeling. It is no accident that poetry is the oldest discursive symbolic form because the poets of pre-literate cultures were the keepers of cultural knowledge, a cultural knowledge that still mingled physical reality in the spoken word with that tendency toward higher levels of abstraction towards which discursive symbolic forms must evolve. Of particular use here are the concepts of *metonymy* and *synecdoche*.

Literary critic Kenneth Burke (1969) identifies metonymy and synecdoche as two of four "Master Tropes" of language—the key functions of discursive symbolism that allow it to work (Burke, 1969: 503-517). Metonymy refers to the ability of words to substitute for physical things. Synecdoche refers to the ability of words to represent physical things. Both terms also underscore the ability of symbolic forms to reduce the totality of an experience to its essence and then communicate that essence to another member of the culture who has learned or is learning how to reanimate that communication once again into a full-fledged experience. Thus, the poet uses her or his aesthetics to reduce the feeling-state of, say, sorrow to a set of expressions that then evokes sorrow in the reader or receiver, or in Langer's terminology, the virtual participant in the poem's sorrow.

If we take Burke, to use an expression, literally, then we might accept that all symbolic forms reduce the totality of the sender's experience into an essence of meaning that can be effectively transferred to another member of the culture through the conduit of that form. In Shotokan karate, this distillation of experience forms the aesthetic, culturally-based knowledge of the physical world that Funakoshi had grasped and concretized into the movements of his style. When we practice Shotokan, it is toward the ultimate end of attempting to reanimate and physically experience that aesthetic. Put another way, we seek to travel through the martial techniques to a higher level of artistic awareness, experience, and understanding.

For the ethnographer, participation in Shotokan karate offers a distinctively emic or "hands-on" methodology of participant observation with a twist. In adopting Langer's orientation to symbolic forms, the ethnographer karateka seeks embodiment of Japanese cultural knowledge as it is embedded in the aesthetic of Funakoshi's system. But unlike some emic study, the purpose of this participation is not to observe and understand; it is to become. The non-discursive symbolic experience does not "mean" something; it is something. Karate does not stand for some sense of the world we can describe with words. Karate stands for some aesthetic sense of the world that we describe in the act of doing karate. In a way, we seek a fleeting moment of illumination and transcendent understanding in the execution of a technique that moves beyond the martial application and allows us to feel a physical experience of artistic expression. That is why karateka hear what their sensei is saying but understand him or her only after accomplishing the technique, often after countless hours of trying to "figure it out." Once realized, the feeling, the experience, of knowledge is remembered kinesthetically and each new attempt at the technique is measured against this non-discursive edge. The challenge for the intercultural anthropologist is to try to identify which elements of non-discursive understanding are based in the culture of the host style and which elements of non-discursive understanding are resident in the alien karateka.

The exciting thing, for me anyway, is that if Ong and Burke are right, then pretty much all of the non-discursive knowledge the Westerner obtains will be from the culture of the host style. Since all Westerners, at least since learning to read, are trapped in the tautology of literacy, we might infer that the only non-discursive knowledge we can assimilate is what another culture, in this case, Japanese culture, provides in the aesthetic of karate study.

Sensei Tanaka prepares to demonstrate a technique to a mixed class of Asian and Anglo students. *Photo courtesy of Andy Timan, Sandan, South Atlantic Karate Association, ISKF-JKA.*

> "the martial arts provide one forum
> well-suited to the needs of scholars
> to identify culturally specific knowledge
> embedded in the act of doing."

Conclusion

Of course, language remains a key to unlocking any culture. Nearly all martial art students realize that the teachings of their respective style is conducted through the medium of their native language. Since this is not the language of the creators of the style, it is inevitable that non-discursive intercultural exchange available via martial arts study will be a slow process. But as we seek to identify and explore cultures different from our own, Langer's theories of non-discursive symbolism help us to understand better the parameters of such tools as *emic* ("hands-on" methodology of participant observation) and *etic* observation. The etic perspective of rational and detached analysis is not only more traditionally objective but clearly limits both the student of martial arts and the ethnographer to the interpretations of culture available through the symbolic form of language. The emic perspective on the other hand, with its emphasis on doing and living in the moment of cultural experience (i.e., non-discursive cultural study) offers exciting possibilities for examining intercultural exchange. But it is also difficult to know, at least in the case of karate, where the physical rigor and dexterity of the discipline impedes access to culture-specific aesthetic awareness. Conscious consideration of this and other limitations, though, can arm the ethnographer karateka with patience and direction. Happily for students of the martial arts, the desire to learn, regardless of how the intercultural exchange occurs, provides us with a guiltless and professional reason to spend a few more hours in training.

REFERENCES

Burke, K. (1968). *Counter-statement*. Berkeley: University of California Press.

Burke, K. (1969). *A grammar of motives*. Berkeley: University of California Press.

Fisher, W. (1984). Narrative as a human communication paradigm: The case for public moral argument. *Communication Monographs* 51, 1-22.

Hershey, L. (1989). Narrative and the creation of place: Narrative elements and cultural identity in Shotokan ritual. *Anthropology and Humanism Quarterly* 14(3), 97-102.

Langer, S. (1980). *Philosophy in a new key* (3rd ed.). Cambridge: Harvard University Press.

Langer, S. (1953). *Feeling and form*. New York: Charles Scribner and Sons.

Myherhoff, B. (1978). *Number our days*. New York: E. P. Dutton.

Ong, W. (1982). *Orality and literacy*. New York: Methuen.

Sandor, A. (1986). Metaphor and belief. *Journal of Anthropological Research* 42, 101-122.

Spradley, J. (1980). *Participant observation*. Chicago: Holt, Rinehart, and Winston.

chapter 4

Samurai in School:
Ryuha in Traditional Japanese Martial Arts
by H. Paul Varley, Ph.D.

Introductory Remarks [applicable for the Chapters by Hurst and Friday]

Western scholars have long been fascinated by the "way of the samurai" in Japanese history. But their attention has been focussed primarily on the spiritual and philosophical aspects of this way as found, for example, in *Hagakure* and the writings of Yamaga Soko. They have shown relatively little interest in the martial arts, even though these arts are not only fundamental to the samurai profession and way but are themselves imbued with the very spiritual and philosophical qualities that the scholars profess to study.

Although neglected as a subject of inquiry by trained scholars, in the West the martial arts have had no difficulty, particularly since the end of World War II, in attracting those who wish to learn and practice them. On the contrary, the number of non-Japanese joining martial arts groups throughout the world continues to increase annually. Some of these practitioners, inspired by their interest in and love for such arts as judo, aikido, and kendo, have written about them, and today there is a substantial literature on the martial arts in languages other than Japanese. Without attempting to evaluate the quality of this literature, one can observe that as a whole it lacks the kind of systematization of inquiry that scholars, trained in the Japanese language and versed in Japanese history, thought, and religion, would be able to apply to the subject.

The following papers[1] bring together for the first time, to my knowledge, a group of scholars specializing in Japanese history, who are also practitioners of the martial arts, to present studies on aspects of these arts. I express my hope that it signals recognition of the martial arts as a valid and indeed important field of study in Japanese history.

Comments

Cameron Hurst succinctly discusses the characteristics of the martial arts that place them squarely into the category of "artistic ways" (*geido*) along with such familiar arts as Noh, the tea ceremony (*chanoyu*), and flower arranging. A distinctive aspect of many of these ways, as Hurst points out, is the *iemoto* or "family headship" system, which evolved during the Tokugawa period. In the tea ceremony, in which the iemoto system became particularly powerful, the principal reason for the establishment of iemoto lineages in the various tea schools was the commercial desire to control the enormous profits derivable from the ever-mounting demand for instruction in chanoyu. Whereas such instruction had previously been in the form of "total transmission"—that is, the pupil received all rights to both the intangible assets (actual instruction in the tea ceremony) and tangible assets (utensils, costume, logo, etc.) of the master—it became partial transmission. Under the partial transmission arrangement, the student, upon completion of his study, receives a certificate to practice and teach his school's method of chanoyu, but the iemoto retains authority over him and can even rescind the certificate if the student fails to conform to the school's rules and standards.

Kabuki, on the other hand, has not developed an iemoto system. One reason for this is that various kabuki troupes often intermingle in staging large theatrical productions, making it difficult to enforce the rules of any one troupe in the workplace. Another reason is the star system in kabuki. As actors become popular among audiences, directors and producers are obliged to give them increasing latitude in how they choose to perform. An iemoto could not tolerate such star status and freedom of conduct in performance.

By contrast, the Noh theater has an iemoto system. In Noh, plays are performed by small casts from single troupes. But more importantly, Noh is governed by exacting rules of training that I suspect are very similar to the kata of the martial arts that Karl Friday discusses. The Noh actor learns the various roles—old man, woman, warrior—by constant repetition until he has mastered them. To use Friday's words, mastery "cannot be conveyed by overt explanation [but] must be experienced directly."

Kabuki with its star system is an exception among the *geido*. One of the most distinctive features of these artistic ways as a whole is the subordination—usually utter subordination—of the individual and his ego to the art and to the will of the group (e.g., school) as represented by the teacher and/or iemoto. A critical aspect of this has been the preservation through the generations of the fundamental principles, rituals, and lineages of the art.

John Rogers, in writing about Japanese swordsmanship,[2] provides a valuable survey of the kinds of documents—certificates of rank or skill, pledges, catalogues of techniques, etc.—that have been preserved and transmitted in swordsmanship. I am impressed, in reading this survey, with what appears to be the far greater emphasis on the mystique of swordsmanship and its traditions than on how to be a skilled swordsman. If my impression is correct, swordsmanship in this sense is very similar to the other artistic ways that evolved in the medieval age.

I am surprised to learn from Hurst's chapter that few of the martial arts schools have developed iemoto systems. The "authority-intensive, patron-client" type of relationships between teachers and students in the martial arts seem almost ideal for the emergence of iemoto. Let me suggest two possible reasons for the infrequency of iemoto in the martial arts: (1) despite their popularity, the martial arts may not generate the kind of profits that were a critical factor in creating iemoto in, for example, chanoyu; and (2) it would be embarrassing, if not untenable, to have hereditary martial arts iemoto who are inferior in skill to their schools' students. No doubt there are problems regarding differences in skills between iemoto and students in other *geido*, but I doubt that they are as critical as they would be in the martial arts.

Reinier Hesselink discusses a martial art, mounted archery, that did not preserve its traditions well in written form and might have become extinct were it not for the efforts of the eighth Tokugawa shogun, Yoshimune, to revive it in the eighteenth century. Hesselink observes that mounted archery "was thought to be 'a divine art which drives away evil spirits and cleanses all pollution.'" Probably all the artistic ways are to one degree or another influenced by magical beliefs, reflected in purification rituals, the exorcising of demons, and the like. I believe that these magical beliefs represent a fascinating subject of inquiry for scholars of the various artistic ways, including the martial arts.

Paul Varley, Ph.D.
Columbia University

NOTES

[1] These papers were presented at the Association for Asian Studies annual meeting 1993.
[2] The paper presented by John Rogers at the Association for Asian Studies meeting is not included in this issue. He is presently in Japan and plans to update this work for publication at a later date.

chapter 5

RYUHA IN THE MARTIAL AND OTHER JAPANESE ARTS

by G. Cameron Hurst, III, Ph.D.

In Japan, the martial arts (*bugei*) are considered to fall within the category of *geido*, or "artistic ways." There are literally hundreds of forms of geido, but they can be classified into essentially three different types.[1] The first to appear historically were the aristocratic cultural forms created by the nobility from Heian times (794-1185) on. They include the playing of musical instruments, *gagaku* performance, falconry, *kemari* (kickball), and poetry composition, as well as art forms developed later in Muromachi times: Noh, flower arranging, tea ceremony, garden architecture, and others.

The martial arts—archery, swordsmanship, use of the lance, equitation, gunnery, even ninjutsu—comprise the second type of *geido*. The third type is the category of popular culture (*taishu geino*), ranging from mime, puppetry and juggling to musical and dance forms and including comical presentations, recitations, and illustrated storytelling among others. The scope of artistic activities which can be included in *geido* is thus extremely broad.

In this chapter, I would like to discuss Japan's martial arts within the broader context of *geido*, comparing them to *ryuha*, or schools, in other traditional arts. Bugei ryuha exhibit characteristics similar to other forms of cultural expression. They share organizational and ritual aspects designed to foster community and continuity, they transmit their teachings in similar ways, and they also share basically similar methods of instruction.

Organizational and Ritual Aspects of Ryuha

Ryuha are corporate groups controlling a particular asset, in the case of the martial and other arts, mastery of specialized cultural forms. Of various size, they are composed basically of a teacher and his (at least in traditional times) students. Relationships between the ryuha head and his students tended to follow authority-intensive, patron-client relationships. Heads of ryuha often assumed parent-like authority in the lives of their student/disciples, serving not only as teacher and role model but mentor, advisor, or even as go-between in contracting marriages.

Some martial arts ryuha developed fully the iemoto pattern of organization and authority common to Japanese traditional arts, in which successive generations of family members controlled the ryu.[2] But comparatively few bugei schools developed this way. More commonly they split into subgroups, so that there are, for example, at the most conservative estimate, well over seven hundred schools of swordsmanship alone. Uncommon in the martial arts world was the phenomenon of an enormous iemoto organization, such as the Urasenke tea ceremony school in which the iemoto today controls the activities of well over a million and a half students through a far flung network of intermediate licensed instructors.

Bugei ryuha tended to practice total transmission so that an individual who had mastered all the secrets of the ryu was fully certified to instruct his own students.[3] Most often he opened his own dojo and created his own school, slightly different from, although derivative of, the style he learned. The original founder rarely retained control over his students after they mastered his techniques. The pattern was repeated generation after generation. In fact, in martial arts this form of organizational development was far more prevalent than situations like the Yagyu family, which served hereditarily as iemoto of their Yagyu Shinkage-ryu school, maintaining tremendous prestige as official fencing instructors to the Tokugawa house.[4]

As corporate groups, however, martial arts schools shared with other ryuha the same concerns with organization and continuity. There was by Tokugawa times normally a dojo,[5] formal training hall which served as the focus of the group's activity. By the Bakumatsu era (1830-1867) there were sometimes dormitory facilities to house students who had come from other domains to study with the teacher. Rather than iemoto, the commonly employed terms by bugei instructors themselves was *shihan*; while meaning teacher in the broad sense, it bears the sense of exemplar, or model, and is thus often rendered in English as "master."

Training halls in all forms of practice, not simply the martial arts, took on a semi-sacred character, since the term *dojo* originally meant a place where religious instruction was conducted and only later was its use extended to other forms of training. A dojo normally housed a *kamidana*, an altar dedicated to a Shinto deity, or a *butsudan* (Buddhist altar). There was often a portrait of the acknowledged founder or some other symbol dedicated to his honor. Ceremonies, commonly involving the exchange of cups of sake, were solemnly performed before the portrait to award certification of mastery of the ryu secrets.[6] These ritual aspects of the ryu served to enhance the group's corporate consciousness.

Establishing authority was crucial to the reputation of a ryuha. Consequently, they attempted to assert some form of traditional authority from the past.[7] One might assert that an edict from a former Emperor had granted its founder a monopoly over a certain activity. Tea ceremony schools tended to claim connection with Sen no Rikyu, as he became venerated as the saint of tea. Other ryuha claimed divine transmission of their secret teachings from some deity, which functioned essentially as a patron saint.[8] Authority might also be enhanced by alleging transmission of the techniques from a famous historical person, like Minamoto Yoshitsune, or from a shadowy *yamabushi* or miraculous *tengu*. Such transmission of authority from a revered person or deity was normally accounted solemnly in ryuha texts, which were transmitted from each generation to the succeeding ryuha head.

The iemoto himself required personal authority to permanently differentiate his status from that of his pupils, especially in such physical activities as martial arts, where the pupil might, in fact, surpass the master in actual ability. In some ryuha, there might be a ceremonial costume which could be worn only by the iemoto. In the Kanze school of Noh, for example, the piece "Yuminagashi" was originally taught to but one person each generation, the iemoto, and when he performed it, he wore a special costume which clearly established his distinctive position.[9]

Symbols of iemoto authority might also be secret or exclusive items—for example, a special mask, fan, tea bowl, musical instrument, sword, or the like. Thus, the Kikutei family traditionally inherited the famous *biwa* (lute) called "Iwao." Of course, the most crucial symbol of iemoto authority, especially in martial arts ryuha, was the possession of scrolls or other texts explaining the secrets (*hiden, okuden, gokui*, etc.), to which we shall turn in a moment.

Bugei ryuha in Edo times, then, consisted of a head instructor, who was either a member of a family of professional teachers of the art or a legitimate successor within an authoritative line of masters, and his students. Meeting in a semi-sacred dojo, protected by the god of the training hall and containing a solemn portrait of the founder, the members of the ryuha were drawn together in deep association focusing on the mastery of their art. The entire society was stratified, from beginning student to the most advanced senior pupil, who was the master's primary assistant.[10] As with other ryuha, to receive instruction, bugei students normally paid on a monthly basis a set fee that varied over time and among schools. Beyond the regular payment of instructional fees, the students offered special ceremonial gifts (salted fish, sake, etc.) at specific times of the year as a means of displaying respect for their teacher.[11] For his part, besides serving as professional instructor of this craft, the master also provided a myriad of specific services for his students, from arranging marriages to finding employment as instructors. Students stayed with the master through a number of graded ranks, similar to the system of belts widely employed in the martial arts today. The ritual nature of the iemoto system, its authoritarian structure and the mystique of camaraderie, often shrouded in secrecy, made it difficult for students to join and leave at will as is often the case today, when teaching is more often a business than a profession.

Transmission of Ryuha Secret Teachings

The activity learned in any ryuha was considered a serious matter, the art was respected, the iemoto venerated, and the effects practice had upon one's character were thought to be of considerable benefit, especially in the martial arts, which never completely lost the justification that warriors needed to maintain some form of combat readiness.

But ryuha were primarily concerned with the transmission of an important cultural form: chanting, dancing, or swordsmanship. It was a serious endeavor; the responsibilities of both instructor and pupil were informed by a tradition of loyalty to the founder, and group consciousness restrained tendencies towards individualistic indulgence. One did not easily join nor leave a martial arts school. In fact, given the inherent danger of the skill instructors were going to impart to a would-be pupil, entry into the practice of swordsmanship necessitated careful scrutiny of the background of the applicant and normally required the recommendation of a respected third party. In common with other ryuha, moreover, martial arts schools extracted pledges from their students as the process of transmission progressed.

There were a number of ways that the secrets of any ryuha could be transmitted from master to disciple. In medieval times, when fighting skills were still practical, teaching and transmission were primitive, immediate, often ad hoc. Not only were there no texts, but it was generally thought, by way of analogy with many Japanese forms of religious expression, that transmission occurred largely by example, allowing little room for verbalization. This idea—in Japanese the term is *ishin denshin*, or nonverbal understanding which goes, literally, from mind (*shin*) to mind—dates back to the beginning of Buddhist tradition and the esoteric transmission from the historical Buddha to his disciple Kashyapa in the Sermon on Vulture Peak. Texts often refer to this idea by the terms *furyu monji* ("no reliance on the written word") or *kyoge betsuden* ("transmission outside the sutras").[12]

The earliest form of transmission of martial skills was called *kuden* (verbal transmission) as was the case with much esoteric knowledge in early Japan, but by late medieval times verbal instructions were often written in brief form, in texts called *kudensho* ("writings of verbal transmission"). The pre-Edo martial arts kudensho extant in a few schools are quite rudimentary, focusing on recounting legends of the founder of the ryuha. The texts offer little in the way of actual instruction in and explication of techniques. All one finds is a listing of several techniques of the school, usually described by hyperbolic terms—"flying dragon," for example—or simply the names of animals—"monkey," "rat," etc.—which would not be readily understood without actual instruction from the teacher.[13]

By the Edo Period, however, it was customary in all ryuha, including martial arts, to write down the teachings of the school and transmit them formally, usually in scrolls but in some cases in bound volumes, to the successful students. The authority of the ryuha iemoto lay in the absolute supremacy of his technique, at least in theory. He was the creative genius behind the techniques, who, in effect, created his own private law or canon, which became sacred only as it was transmitted by successive iemoto to their disciples.[14] The techniques were written down as *hiden, gokuden, gokui* (secret transmissions) or *tora no maki* ("The Tiger Scroll") and were valued by the students as the embodiment of the wisdom of the ryuha.

Initiation into the secret techniques of the ryuha usually meant the award of a certificate of mastery, a license which carried with it the express right of the initiate to reproduce its forms, whether flower arranging or swordsmanship. Transmission of the ryuha teachings involved several levels or grades. In the martial arts it was common to have eight levels, but there were many schools with five and some were even reduced to three. Consequently, the typical iemoto organization was a hierarchical structure with the iemoto or shihan at the peak. He was the ultimate authority who transmitted the teachings in graded segments to the disciples, awarding certification for mastery of a certain level at an appropriate ceremony. The highest level was normally referred to as *kaiden* ("complete transmission") or *menkyo kaiden* ("certified complete transmission"), the receipt of which in most bugei ryuha qualified one to become an independent teacher in his own right.

Concern for the secrecy of the teachings transmitted was paramount in all organizations, but perhaps of greatest worry to bugei ryuha, since the techniques in which students were being instructed were potentially lethal. Instruction to the wrong kind of person was a problem, and great care was thus exercised by most school heads to accept only pupils of outstanding character. In pre-Edo times, when teaching was barely developed and not yet a profession upon which livelihood depended, instructors were more strict. But even in Tokugawa Japan, students were not automatically accepted without some check on their character.[15] By his behavior, a bad student could severely embarrass the head of a tea ceremony or flower arranging ryuha. But a student who misused the sword or spear to injure or kill someone was a far greater threat to both society and the reputation of the instructor.

Yet concern appears about equally distributed across the iemoto organizations. It was common for all masters to extract pledges and oaths from their students that they would not disclose the secrets of the school nor teach them to others without the explicit authorization of the master. Heads of bugei ryuha, especially swordsmanship, demanded pledges from students at virtually each level of certification." Martial arts pledges were similar in form to those of other ryuha. Called *kishomon*, they were normally sealed with the blood of the one making the pledge and written on special paper which indicated their importance.

The pledges were commonly written on Kumuno goo paper, which came from Kumano Shrine, a series of three venerable Shinto institutions located in what is today Wakayama Prefecture. The *Kumano goo* ("Ox King") was a talisman which became popular in the early medieval period as faith in the deities of the three Kumano shrines soared and they became the object of frequent pilgrimages.[17] Yamabushi and *miko* (female shrine shamans) sold the talismans, which became a craze among pilgrims flocking to Kumano. It was a special sheet of paper on which were inscribed the five Chinese characters *Kumuno gohoin* ("The Honored Treasure Seal of Kumano"). The inscription was written in a strange calligraphy: the characters were composed with small black crows, the crow being considered the messenger of the Kumano deities." The paper was then pressed with the vermilion seal of the shrine. Pasted to door frames, it drove away evil spirits; planted in fields, it scared away birds and the wind; and fixed to a pole in irrigated fields, it supposedly brought a bountiful harvest. As its popularity rose, *Kumano goo* became valued as the major form of paper used by Japan's warrior class in writing a variety of *kishomon*. By the Tokugawa period, it had become the standard paper on which oaths were written to protect the secrets of a ryuha.

Written by the aspiring disciple, the document normally contained an introduction and a number of formulaic phrases which stated that the student would not show to anyone nor tell anyone of the secrets into which he was being initiated, whether it be parent or child, nor would he show the scroll containing the secrets to anyone. All of this would normally appear on a separate sheet, followed by the *Kumano goo* paper, on which he pledged to keep his word, invoking the names of a variety of native and foreign gods. Some invocations were rather brief, but it was more common to be exhaustive, leaving no major deity unmentioned. Here, for example, is a pledge of an archery school.

1) I deem it a great honor to have imparted to me the secrets of the X-ryu.
2) I shall concentrate on my training day and night without remission. If, unfortunately, I have no time to practice, I shall give up the bow.
3) I understand that as I progress in my training you will gradually unfold to me the secrets of your art and that you will regulate my progress not according to the length of my discipleship but according to the skill and accomplishment I display. Realizing this I shall never harbor any resentments against my teacher.
4) The verbal instructions and the written tradition which you give me I will never reveal even to my parents or brothers, much less to anyone else. If it should happen that after receiving the written tradition my house should die out, it shall be immediately burned or returned. It goes without saying that I shall not take pupils of my own until you give me a license to do so.
5) I shall never indulge in criticism of other schools of archery. Should I ever offend against anyone of these rules, may I receive the divine punishment of Hachiman-bosatsu, Bunten, Taishaku, the Four Tenno, all the Great and Lesser Gods of Japan, the Two Gongen of Izu and Hakone, Temman Tenjin and the ancestors of my Clan.

In sign whereof I lay my oath and set my seal.

Pledges were required regardless of the rank or social status of the student. The Yagyu family held iemoto status in the Yagyu Shinkage-ryu throughout the Edo period, serving as hereditary shogunal instructors. And even the shogun was required to make such pledges. Kishomon from shoguns Ieyasu to Ietsuna were written and duly offered to successive Yagyu iemoto, preserved as part of the esoterica passed on from one head to his successor.

Philosophy ad Methods of Instruction

The martial arts share with other *geido* the characteristic of being a way of personally experiencing an art form. They involve, according to Nishiyama, actions which "create or recreate cultural value through the exercise of the whole body or a part thereof—dancing, performing, drawing, sniffing, tasting, speaking, playing, and so forth."[20] While the actions do result in some form of cultural product, these products are normally formless, rather than objectified. That is, the resultant *product* is less important than the *process*: the value for the individual lies in the doing, the playing, performing, singing, etc. In this creation through the actions of the body, technique (*waza*) is of primary importance. One must strive to develop the ability to perform requisite techniques to perfection. This concern for mastery of technique lies at the heart of every form of *geido*, from swordsmanship to tea ceremony.

In order to master the techniques of some art such as swordsmanship, it was crucial to select a good teacher. Accordingly, *geido* instructors exhibited serious concern for their reputations. A swordsmanship instructor could gain a reputation, at least through the early Edo period, by means of popular recognition of his successful duels or the record of battles in which he had distinguished himself. Another way was simply to rely upon the weight of tradition, as the iemoto of a well-known professional ryuha. And of course in Edo times, especially in the mid to late period, a teacher could win a reputation for successfully defeating other skilled fencers in *taryu jiai*.[21]

The instructor enjoyed almost absolute power over the student in any discipline, whether it be fencing or the tea ceremony. His authority was supreme, his word unquestioned. But contemporary educational philosophy held that the instructor was of limited use; he was only an imperfect guide to personal mastery of the techniques involved. The master conveyed the waza to the student, who through sheer repetition would ultimately, at least in theory, reach a perfect understanding himself. And despite the production of numerous texts in Tokugawa times which describe the various waza and the forms (*kata*), which were the actual vehicles for studying, the tradition that true understanding could not be conveyed verbally or through instructional manuals but only nonverbally, through experience (*ishin denshin*), never died.

Many forms of Japanese Buddhism, from Tendai through Zen, emphasized an esoteric transmission from master to disciple. In that sense, the iemoto of any bugei or other ryuha instructed his disciples in a manner analogous to that of many religious masters.

In fact, early Japanese texts are replete with words which emphasize that the realization of meaning of the techniques is a non-intellectual process but one of total bodily understanding that can only be experienced. They include such terms as *taitoku* ("to obtain with the body"), *taikan* ("to experience through the body"), or *tainin* ("to understand with the body"). This is often expressed more colloquially by the phrase "to learn with the body" (*shintai de oboeru* or *karada de oboeru*).[22]

The type of practice espoused by the martial and other arts that was in all *geido* of medieval and early modern times was commonly called *keiko*. While it can be broadly understood as meaning "to learn," the term is an ancient Chinese expression first used in Japan in the Kojiki in the four character compound *keiko shokon*,[23] literally "to reflect upon past ways to shed light on the present." Thus the distinct meaning of keiko was to take the past as precedent, but in medieval Japan it came to be applied almost exclusively to learning outside pure intellectual study, specifically for the study of *geido*. As used in texts dealing with poetic composition, flower arranging, and of course swordsmanship, keiko took on the sense of learning which requires polishing through repetition of established forms—a positive, engaged learning as opposed to a passive acceptance of received written material.

There was also a certain attitudinal, or spiritual, sense about the term "keiko." Keiko was more than an intellectual understanding of a body of material; it was intimately linked to own's mental attitude (*kokorogamae*) and involved a concern for the way one ought to live. In both a Confucian and a

Buddhist sense, keiko meant to learn the proper way of living (*do*) through mastery of one's art form. The English term "training" may be the most appropriate translation of keiko, which even today is the commonly used term to describe the process one goes through when he or she enters a study of tea, flowers, poetry, dance, judo or any of the traditional arts. In keiko the emphasis is heavily upon the character and the totality of personal development: mastery of the way of tea, for example, as a means of personal fulfillment and development.

Keiko learning focused upon the mastery of *kata* (forms) which taught the disciple waza. Since all *geido* had a kata focus, many scholars have defined the Japanese cultural tradition as the "culture of kata."[24] Among the bugei, archery developed a kata tradition quite early, but with most martial arts it was in the late medieval period that people began to teach individual battlefield skills as specific techniques. Then a number of military geniuses created kata, based on their long years of military experience, as fixed ways of practicing necessary combat skills.

It was in the teaching of these highly individualistic technique that specific ryuha emerged. Kata became the rules, the basic methods, by which techniques were transmitted from master to student within the ryu. It was believed that kata most quickly and completely imparted the techniques to the students. The method of instruction was simply to repeat, over and over again, the kata under the guidance of the master. Learning involved a rote imitation of the teacher's kata, with no resistance, no attempt to embellish, and commonly with no explanation of the individual moves. Constant polishing of the moves, inner reflection on the process, down to the tiniest detail of stance or how one held one's hands, it was believed, would ultimately result in an understanding—again through the body, which included the mind—not only of the teacher's techniques but also of the requisite spirit as well.

Geido in Japan today preserve thousands of kata which were originally developed by the founders of ryuha, altered and improved over the centuries and handed down until the present, as the most appropriate ways of mastering such diverse cultural activities as swordsmanship and Noh performance. The iemoto enjoys almost total control over the students, who are subjected to intensive training in the no-questions-asked repetition of fixed forms until the teacher deems progress sufficient for them to move on to another stage. It seems peculiarly antiquated and out of step with the freedom and individualism of modern educational ideas. But the tyranny of kata training is ironic insofar as total submission to authority is regarded as the best way to reach individual creativity.[25]

Kata mastery was regarded as progressing through three stages. One finds throughout *geido* texts reference to *shu, ha,* and *ri,* a sequence of developmental steps to mastery.[26] *Shu* means "to preserve" and refers to the initial phase of study in martial and other arts. In this stage the novice simply "preserves" the tradition by constant repetition of kata, polishing both outward form and internal mental awareness until the waza become automatically replicable, whether it be the ability to use a sword effortlessly or throw a pot with no conscious effort. But there was concern that simple repetition ultimately could (and certainly did in Edo period martial arts) lead to the ossification of the art, so the student must "break down" or "destroy" (*ha*) the kata he has mastered in order to move to the final stage of development where he was "liberated" (*ri*) from the kata and true creative individuality could express itself.

守破離

shu - ha - ri

Of course, the number of people able to achieve mastery through a progression from *shu* through *ha* to *ri* is quite limited, both historically and currently as well. It was exceedingly difficult to reach mastery in many of the traditional *geido*. For example, 1,384 people entered the Yabuuchi-ryu of tea ceremony during the Edo period and only eleven reached the pinnacle of kaiden rank.[27] Nonetheless, the theory behind the mastery of secrets via kata memorization involved a progression from total subservience to tradition to a level of individualistic creativity.

The Japanese traditionally regard keiko instruction as being very rigorous. Although many of the traditional arts were recreational, creative activities for leisure time (and are practiced as such today—tea ceremony for brides, kendo for kiddies), there was and still is an expectation that the student will give total devotion to the "way" of that art. Martial arts texts, for example, are full of terms such as *shisshin* ("devotion"), *doshin* ("devotion to the way," literally "way-mind"), and the like. The idea was that the student devote himself exclusively and totally to the mastery of the kata of the particular endeavor. In an almost a religious sense, one should cut himself off from the secular world and enter his art world; he should find the time (*hima*) to concentrate on his art so that, sleeping or waking, every moment is devoted to mastery.[28]

Zeami said it for all *geido* in his discussion of the attitude required in mastering Noh: "He who would attain this Way must not engage in the non-Way."[29] What he meant by "non-Way" was any other activity, other form of learning or art form. This single-minded devotion to the particular way one chose was widely advocated among all the *geido* and is especially common in martial arts texts. The idea is that if one devotes himself exclusively to the total understanding of a single way, then paradoxically, that understanding is consistent across all ways. Miyamoto Musashi, for example, claimed that after years of devoting himself single-mindedly to *heiho* (martial arts), he ultimately came to be conversant with a variety of *geido*, all without the aid of a teacher.[30]

FOOTNOTES

[1] Nishiyama Matsunosuke, "Kinsei geido shiso-no tokushitsu to sono tenkai," in *Kinsei geidoron*, Vol. 61 in *Nihon shiso taikei*, (Tokyo: Iwanami Shoten, 1972), pp. 589-92.

[2] On iemoto systems, see O'Neill, P. G., "Organization and authority in the traditional arts," *Modern Asian Studies*, Vol. 18, No. 3 (1984), pp. 631-645.

[3] Nishiyama Matsunosuke, "Kinsei no yugeiron," in *Kinsei geidoron*, op. cit., p. 618.

[4] Ibid. The reason for this pattern of discontinuity in authority was apparently the closed nature of the society, in which the bakufu jealously discouraged too much association among warriors of various domains. It would have been virtually impossible, for example, for a swordsman from a Kyushu domain to learn swordsmanship at a Yagyu family dojo in Edo and return to his domain and remain under the authority of the Yagyu iemoto. Thus, an extensive swordsmanship ryuha which organized warriors from different fiefs along strict iemoto lines was unimaginable for most of the Tokugawa period although in Bakumatsu times it was much more common for bushi from different *han* to train together in a common dojo. And it led to precisely what the bakufu feared: inter-*han* plotting against the shogunate. iemoto organizations were more common in domain fencing schools, where the clientele was limited to samurai of one domain.

[5] For information on dojo, see Tominaga Kengo, *Kendo gohyakunen shi*, (Tokyo: Hyakusen Shobo, 1972), pp. 409-15. Prior to the Tokugawa period, martial arts like swordsmanship were practiced largely outdoors where actual battle conditions could be approximated. But in the peaceful Tokugawa era, as martial skills became martial arts, and especially in late Edo times, when individual competitive matches became popular, fencing increasingly took place in dojo. They ranged in size from very tiny ones—the Yoshikawa family dojo, where Tsukahara Bokuden practiced in

Kashima, is so small one cannot raise a sword fully over his head—to magnificent ones in Edo, like the Nakanishi school with some fifteen *ken* of wooden floor (one *ken* is just short of one yard).

6   Nakabayashi Shinji, "Kendoshi," in *Nihon budo taikei*, (Tokyo: Dobosha, 1982), Vol. 10, p. 45.

7   Nishiyama Matsunosuke, *Zemoto no kenkyu*, (Tokyo: Yoshikawa Kobunkan, 1982), pp. 83-4.

8   The most famous of the swordsmanship ryuha with such connections were, of course, associated with Kashima and Katori shrines.

9   Nishiyama, *Zemoto no kenkyu*, p. 77. In all forms of cultural performance, but perhaps especially in such physically demanding endeavors as martial arts, it was not unlikely that the student might have greater ability than the teacher. Thus, special mechanisms were established—family-transmitted teachings, special clothing or ritual implements, and the like—to allow even untalented masters authority over their students.

10 Interestingly, ryuha even functioned as arenas of social mobility in strictly stratified Tokugawa Japan. Most expert fencers in late Tokugawa Japan tended to be lower-ranking samurai often blocked from advancement by the severe restrictions in warrior society or by ronin without prospects in society or even by commoners, a number of whom rose to head their own dojo and even serve as instructors to daimyo. Many achieved a degree of status based upon actual achievement—the demonstration of physical superiority over others—denied them in other social arenas.

As was the case in other cultural forms, fencers, archers, and other martial artists often took special ceremonial names. Martial arts genealogies bristle with names such as Sekishasai, Ryounsai, Ikosai, Ren'yasai, so-called *saimei* which apparently were adopted after one had officially taken Buddhist vows. Such names afforded a degree of recognition within the special world of the ryuha. But even without special names, demonstrated expertise in such endeavors as swordsmanship, the tea ceremony, or some other art conferred prestige and buttressed self-esteem. For a Tokugawa vassal of low rank who never achieved any success as a retainer, for example, Katsu Kokichi took extraordinary pride in his achievements in the world of fencing, where he had few peers. It was one arena in which he could prove himself. See Katsu Kokichi, *Musui's story: The autobiography of a Tokugawa samurai*, (Tuscon, Arizona: University of Arizona Press, 1988), passim.

11 Most schools had written rules and regulations, often referred to as *kokoroe no koto* (literally, "things to be understood"), which included matters of financial consideration. See, for example, the *Nyujuku kokoroe no koto* of

the famous Shinto Munen-ryu Renbeikan of Otani Seiichiro in *Nihon budo zenshu*, (Tokyo: Jimbutsu Oraisha, 1967), p. 152.

[12] Nakabayashi Shinji, "Nihon kobudo ni okeru shintairon," *Riso*, No. 604, September, 1983, p. 109. (Hereafter, "Shintairon.")

[13] Thus, a text might be extremely brief, listing the names of techniques, followed by the words "verbally transmitted" (*kuden*).

[14] Nishiyama Matsunosuke, *Iemoto no kenkyu*, pp. 24-5.

[15] The personal relationship between master and student was considered important from the moment the student entered the instructor's charge. Usually accompanied by his parents and in formal dress, the would-be fencing or other martial arts student (age of entry ranged from around nine or ten to mid-teens) visited the school for a formal meeting with the instructor, presented an appropriate registration present (*sokushu*)— usually fans or writing brushes—and signed a pledge to study hard under the master's tutelage and keep the teachings secret. Tominaga, *Kendo gohyakunen-shi*, pp. 40 1-2.

[16] Nakabayashi, "Kendoshi," p. 45.

[17] "Kumano goo," entry in *Nihon rekishi duijiten*, (Tokyo: Kawade Shobo, 1968), Vol. 4, pp. 95-6.

[18] Ibid, p. 96.

[19] Quoted in Ronald P. Dore, *Education in Tokugawa Japan*, (Berkeley and Los Angeles: University of California Press, 1965), pp. 149-50.

[20] Nishiyama Matsunosuke, "Kinsei geido shiso no tokushitsu to sono tenkai," in *Kinsei geidoron*, pp. 585-6.

[21] *Taryu jiai*, literally "contests with other schools," were strictly forbidden for most of the Edo period (1600-1868), but during the Bakumatsu (1830-1867), they became quite common, even attracting crowds of onlookers.

[22] Nakabayashi, "Shintairon," p. 114.

[23] Nakabayashi Shinji, "Budo no susume, 6: Keiko ni tsuite," *Budo*, April 1986, pp. 12-13.

[24] Nishiyama, "Kinsei geido shiso," p. 586.

[25] Nakabayashi Shinji, "Budo no susume, 5: Budo no tokusei 'kata,'" *Budo*, March 1986, pp. 14.5.

[26] Nakabayashi, "Shintairon," p. 114.

[27] Nishiyama, *Iemoto no kenkyu*, p. 40.

[28] Nakabayashi, "Budo no susume, 6," p. 13.

[29] Quoted in ibid.

[30] Miyamoto Musashi, Sorin no sho, in *Nihon budo taikei*, Vol. 2, p. 52.

chapter 6

KABALA IN MOTION:
KATA AND PATTERN PRACTICE
IN THE TRADITIONAL BUGEI
by Karl F. Friday, Ph.D.

The term *ryuha*, prosaically translated as "school," can be more literally and more evocatively rendered as "branch of the current." The current here represents the onward flow of a stream of thought—an approach to martial art—through time; the branches betoken the partitioning of those teachings, the splitting off that occurs as insights are passed from master to students, generation after generation. Ryuha do not exist to foster skill in combat and the use of weaponry, but to hand on knowledge. For skill cannot be taught or learned; it can only be acquired, through long training and practice; and can be gained nearly as readily without as with a teacher who has himself mastered the art. Skill is, for the most part, self-discovered, imposed on the student from within his own aptitude and discipline. But knowledge can be bequeathed. The perceptions, inspirations, experiences and wisdom collected over the course of a lifetime by a master of an art can be imparted to students so that each generation can build on the privity of those that came before and each new student will not have to begin the process of discovery from scratch.

The essence of a ryuha, then, can be found in the transmission of its kabala. The essence of that transmission can be found in *kata*, the oldest and still the central methodology for teaching and learning the body of knowledge that constitutes a traditional ryuha.

Few facets of Japanese martial art have been as consistently and ubiquitously misunderstood, even by those who practice them, as kata. Variously described as a kind of ritualized combat; exercises in aesthetic movement; a means to sharpen fundamentals, such as balance and coordination; a type of moving meditation; or a form of training akin to shadow-boxing, kata embraces elements of all these characterizations, but its essence is captured by none of them. Kata, in fact, defies succinct explanation.

The standard English translation for "*kata*" is "form" or "forms," but while this is linguistically accurate, the nature and function of kata are better conveyed by the phrase "pattern practice." Fundamentally, kata represents a training method wherein students rehearse combinations of techniques and counter-techniques, or sequences of such combinations, arranged by their teachers. In most cases, students work in pairs.[1] One partner is designated as the attacker or opponent and is called the *uchitachi* (when he uses a sword), *uchite* (when he uses any other weapon), or *ukete* (when he is unarmed). The other employs the techniques the kata is designed to teach and is called the *shitachi* (in sword training) or the *shite* (when training unarmed or with other weapons).

This sort of pattern practice provides continuity with the ryuha from generation to generation, even in the absence of written instruments for transmission. The kata practiced by a given ryuha can and do change from generation to generation—or even within the lifetime of an individual teacher—but they are normally considered to have been handed down intact by the founder or some other important figure in the school's heritage. "In order," observed Edo period commentator Fujiwara Yoshinobu, "to transmit the essence of the school [*ryugi no honshitsu*] to later generations, one must teach faithfully, in a manner not in the slightest different from the principles [*jiri*] of the previous teachers."[2] Changes, when they occur, are viewed as being superficial, adjustments to the outward form of the kata; the key elements—the marrow—of the kata do not change. By definition, more fundamental changes (when they are made intentionally and acknowledged as such) connote the branching off of a new ryuha.[3]

The Nature of Kata and Pattern Practice

One of the key points to be understood about pattern practice in the traditional bugei is that it serves as the core of training and transmission. In modern Japanese martial arts, such as kendo or judo, kata is often only one of several more or less co-equal training methods, but in the older ryuha, pattern practice was and is the pivotal method. Many schools teach only through pattern practice. Others employ adjunct learning devices, such as sparring, but only to augment kata training, never to supplant it.

The importance of pattern practice comes from the belief that it is the most efficient vehicle for passing knowledge from teacher to student. On one level, a ryuha's kata form a living catalog of its curriculum and a syllabus for instruction. Both the essence and the sum of a ryuha's teachings—the postures, techniques, strategies, and philosophy that comprise a school's kabala—are contained in its kata. And the sequence in which students are taught the kata is usually fixed by tradition and/or by the headmaster of the school. In this way, pattern practice is a means to systematize and regularize training. But the real function of kata goes far beyond this.

Mastery of the bugei or other traditional Japanese arts is a suprarational process. The most important lessons cannot be conveyed by overt explanation; they must be experienced directly. The essence of a ryuha's kabala can never be fully expounded; it must be intuited from examples in which it is put into practice. David Slawson, discussing the art of gardening, describes traditional learning as taking place through an "osmosis-like process, through the senses, with little theorizing [about] the underlying principles."[4] His observations echo those of a late Tokugawa period commentator on the bugei:

> Theory [narai] is not to be taught lightly; it is to be passed on a little at a time to those who have achieved merit in practice, in order to help them understand the principles [of the art]. Theory, even if not taught, will develop spontaneously with the accumulation of correct training.[5]

The role of the teacher in the bugei tradition, then, is to serve as model and guide, not as lecturer or conveyor of information. The standard appellation for teachers of traditional arts, *shihan*, reflects this role. Although commonly translated as "instructor" or "master instructor," the term literally means something more on the order of "master and model." Bugei teachers lead students along the path to mastery of their arts; they do not tutor them. Issai Chozan's early eighteenth century classic text on swordsmanship, *Keko no myojutsu*, concludes with an eloquent statement of this principle:

> The teacher only transmits the technique and illuminates its principle. To acquire its truth is within oneself. [In Zen Buddhism] this is called self-attainment; or it may also be called mind-to-mind transmission or special transmission outside the texts. Learning in this fashion does not subvert the doctrines [of the texts], for even a teacher could not transmit [in that way]. Nor is such learning found only in the study of Zen, for in the meditations of the Confucian sages and in all of the arts, mastery

lies in mind-to-mind transmission, special transmission outside the texts. Texts and doctrine merely point to what one already has within oneself but cannot see on one's own. Understanding is not bestowed by the teacher. Teaching is easy; listening to doctrines is also easy; but to find with certainty what is within oneself, to make this one's own, is difficult. [In Zen] this is called seeing one's nature. Enlightenment is an awakening from the dream of delusion; it is the same as understanding. This does not change.[6]

To say that understanding comes from within the student should not, however, imply that mastery of the martial (or other) arts mostly involves some mystical discovery of truths preexisting but buried within the self or some magical bursting forth of the learner's inner being. Quite the contrary, bugei instruction prescribes a gradual, developmental process in which teachers help students to internalize the key of ryuha doctrine. Understanding and mastery of these precepts comes from within, the result of the student's own efforts. But the teacher presents the precepts and creates an environment in which the student can absorb and comprehend them from without.[7] The overall process can be likened to teaching a child to ride a bicycle: the child does not innately know how to balance, pedal and steer, nor will he be likely to discover how on his own. At the same time, no one can fully explain any of these skills either; one can only demonstrate them and help the child practice them until he figures out for himself which muscles are doing what at which times to make bicycle riding possible.

To fully appreciate the function of pattern practice as a teaching and learning device, it is important to understand just what it is that is supposed to be taught and learned and the relationship of this knowledge to kata. The essential knowledge—the kabala—of a ryuha can be broken down into three components: *hyoho* or *heiho* ("strategy"), *te-no-uchi* ("skill" or "application of skill"), and *waza* ("techniques" or "tactics"). *Hyoho* refers to something along the lines of "the essential principles of martial art," wherein "essential" is taken in its original meaning of "that which constitutes the essence." As such, hyoho designates the general principles upon which the ryuha's approach to combat is constructed: the rationale for choosing between defensive or offensive tactics, the angles of approach to an opponent, the striking angles and distances appropriate to various weapons, the proper mental posture to be employed in combat, the goals to be sought in combat, and similar considerations. Te-no-uchi constitute the fundamental skills required for the application of *hyoho*, such as timing, posture, the generation and concentration of power, and the like. Waza are the situationally specific applications of a ryuha's *hyoho* and *te-no-uchi*, the particularized tactics in and through which a student is trained. Waza, *te-no-uchi*, and *hyoho* are functionally inseparable; *hyoho* is manifested in and by waza through *te-no-uchi*.

Kata, then, are compendiums of waza and, as such, are manifestations of all three components. More importantly, they are the means by which a student learns and masters first *te-no-uchi* and then *hyoho*. As Fujiwara Yoshinobu observed:

> Technique and principle are indivisible, like a body and its shadow; but one should emphasize the polishing of technique. The reason for this is that principle will manifest itself spontaneously in response to progress in technical training. One should vociferously stifle any impulses to verbally debate principle.[8]

In emphasizing ritualized pattern practice and minimizing analytical explanation, bugei masters blend ideas and techniques from the two educational models most familiar to medieval and early modern Japanese warriors: Confucianism and Zen. Kata training first of all shares elements in common with the Zen traditions of *ishin-denshin*, or "mind-to-mind transmission" and what Victor Hori terms "teaching without teaching." The former stresses the importance of a student's own immediate experience over explicit verbal or written explanation, engaging the deeper layers of a student's mind and bypassing the intellect; the latter describes a learning tool applied in Rinzai monasteries whereby students are assigned jobs and tasks that they are expected to learn and perform expertly with little or no formal explanation. Both force the student to fully invoke his powers of observation, analysis and imagination in order to comprehend where he is being steered. Both lead to a level of understanding beyond cognition of the specific task or lesson presented.[9]

But learning through pattern practice probably derives most directly from Confucian pedagogy and its infatuation with ritual and ritualized action. This infatuation is predicated on the conviction that through action and practice, man fashions the conceptual frameworks he uses to order—and thereby comprehend—the chaos or raw experiences of life. One might describe, explain, or even defend one's perspectives by means of analysis and rational argument, but one cannot acquire them in this way. Ritual is stylized action, sequentially structured experience that leads those who follow it to wisdom and understanding. Those who seek knowledge and truth, then, must be carefully guided through the right kind of experience if they are to achieve the right kind of understanding. For the early Confucians, whose principal interest was the proper ordering of the state and society, this meant habitualizing themselves to the codes of what they saw as the perfect political organization, the early Zhou dynasty (1122?-256 B.C.E.). For bugei students, it means ritualized duplication of the actions of past masters.[10]

In point of fact, Confucian models dominated all aspects of traditional samurai education, not just the bugei—particularly the Zhu Xi Neo-Confucian concept of investigating the abstract through the concrete and the general through the particular, but also the Wang Yangming (Oyomei) version of Neo-Confucianism's emphasis on the necessity of unifying knowledge and action.[11] The central academic subjects of such an education were calligraphy and the reading of the Confucian classic texts in Chinese. Calligraphy was taught almost entirely by setting students to copy models provided by their teacher. Students would repeatedly practice brushing out characters that imitated as closely as possible those that appeared in their copy books as the teacher moved from student to student to observe and offer corrections. Reading, too, was to be learned through what Ronald Dore describes as "parrot-like repetition."[12] After the teacher slowly read off a short passage- usually no more than four or five characters and at most half a page—from the text, students were directed to recite the passage over and over again for themselves until they had mastered its form. Once this was achieved, the teacher would offer some general idea of the meaning of the passage, and the students would return to their practice. Such instruction formed virtually the whole of a young student's first five to seven years of training. The method showed little concern for comprehension of contents and offered little or no systematic analysis or explanation of even the principles of Chinese grammar and syntax or of the meanings of individual characters. Rather, it was expected that once acquainted with enough examples, the student would acquire the principles underlying them in gestalt-like fashion. The idea was that learning to recite texts in this fashion was a necessary preparatory step to true reading. Having mastered the former, the student at length moved on to the latter, revisiting the same Confucian classics he had been struggling through for years but now with the goal of comprehending their meaning rather than just their form. Toward this end, teachers offered lectures and written commentaries on the texts, but the principal pedagogical tool was still individual practice and repetition interspaced with regular sessions, in which the teacher would quiz students on difficult passages and incite them to work their way through them.[13]

In the light of this, the value medieval and early modern Japanese bugei instructors placed on kata should hardly be surprising. But the notion that "ritual formalism"—in which "students imitate form without necessarily understanding content or rationale"—can lead to deeper understanding and spontaneity of insight than rational instruction—in which the teacher attempts to articulate the general principles of a task and transmit these to students—is not entirely foreign to Western education either, as Victor Hori observes:

> As a graduate student in philosophy, I taught propositional logic to first- and second-year university students and noticed that the class divided into two groups, those who could solve the logic problems and those who could not. Those who could solve them started by memorizing the basic transformation formulae of propositional logic. . . . Having committed these formulae to memory, these students were thereby able to solve the logic problems because they could "just see" common factors in the equations and then cancel them out, or could "just see" logical equivalences. However, the other students, those who had not committed the transformation formulae to memory, were more or less mystified by the problems though many made serious attempts to "reason" their way through. . . . those who had done the rote memory work had developed logical insight.[14]

Pattern practice in Japanese bugei also bears some resemblance to medieval Western methods of teaching painting and drawing, in which art students first spent years copying the works of old masters, learning to imitate them perfectly before venturing on to original works of their own. Through this copying, they learned and absorbed the secrets and principles inherent in the masters' techniques without consciously analyzing or extrapolating them. In like manner, kata are the "works" of a ryuha's current and past masters, the living embodiment of the school's teachings. Through their practice, a student makes these teachings a part of him and later passes them on to students of his own.

It is important, however, not to lose sight of the fact that kata are a means to mastery of a ryuha's kabala, expressions of that kabala; they are not the kabala itself. Mastery of pattern practice is not the same as mastery of the art; a student's training begins with pattern practice, but it is not supposed to end there. Kata are not, for example, intended to be used as a kind of database mechanically applied to specific combat situations ("when the opponent attacks with technique 7-A, respond with counter-technique 7-A-1, unless he is left-handed, in which case. . ."). Rather, pattern practice is employed as a tool for teaching and learning the principles that underlie the techniques that make up the kata. Once these principles have been absorbed, the tool is to be set aside.

Viewed, then, from the perspective of a student's lifetime, pattern practice is a temporary expedient in his training and development. The eventual goal is for the student to move beyond codified, technical applications to express the essential principles of the art in his own unique fashion, to transcend both the kata and the waza from which they are composed, just as art students moved beyond imitation and copying to produce works of their own.[15]

As he moves toward mastery of the ryuha's teachings, the bugei student's relationship with his school's kata evolves through three stages, expressed by some authorities as "Preserve, Break, and Separate" (*mamoru, yabureru, hanareru,* or *shu-ha-ri*). In the first stage he attempts to merge himself into the kata, to bury his individuality within its confines. He is made to imitate the movements and postures of his teachers exactly and is allowed no departure from the ordained pattern. When he has been molded to the point where it is difficult for him to move or react in any fashion outside the framework of the kata, he is pushed on to the next stage, where he consciously seeks to break down this framework and step outside it. He experiments with variations on the patterns he has been taught, probing their limits and boundaries and in the process sharpening and perfecting his grasp of the principles that underlie the forms. Only when he has accomplished this can he move on the final stage, the stage of true mastery. Here he regains his individuality. Whereas previously he merged himself into the kata, he now emerges fused with the kabala of the ryuha. He moves freely, unrestricted by the framework of the kata, but his movements and instincts are wholly in harmony with those of the kata.

Historical Problems and Criticisms of Kata and Pattern Practice

Pattern practice is a time-honored and, when properly conducted, an efficacious means of training and transmission of knowledge, but it is not without pitfalls. It is easy to imagine that a methodology centered on imitation and rote memorization could readily degenerate into stagnation and empty formalism. The historical record indicates that this was already becoming a problem for *bugei ryuha* in Japan by the late seventeenth century.

Certificates of achievement and similar documents left by fifteenth and sixteenth century martial art masters suggest that kata had become the principle means of transmission by this time.[16] It was not, however, the only way in which warriors learned how to fight. Most bushi built on insights gleaned from pattern practice with experience in actual combat. This was, after all, the "Age of the Country at War," when participation in battles was both the goal and the motivation for training. Moreover, a number of the most illustrious swordsmen of the age, including Tsukahara Bokuden, Kamiizumi Ise-no-kami, Miyamoto Mushashi, Yagyu Muneyoshi, Yagyu Hyogosuke, and Ito Kagehisa, are known to have traveled about the country seeking instruction and engaging in duels and sparring matches, a practice, known as *musha shugyo*, which many authorities believe to have been common among serious bugei students. Ordinarily, such students would begin their instruction with a teacher near their home, train with him until they had absorbed all they could, and then set out on the road, offering and accepting challenges from practitioners of other styles. Warriors defeated in such matches (if they survived unmaimed) often became the students of those who bested them.[17]

Training conditions altered considerably in the decades after the battle of Sekigahara in 1600. First, the new Tokugawa shogunate placed severe restrictions on the freedom of samurai to travel outside their own domains. Second, the teaching of martial arts began to emerge as a profession. Adepts no longer divided their energies between training students and participation in war as there were no longer wars in which to participate. Instead, they began to open training halls and devote themselves full-time to instructing students, who paid fees for their training. And third, contests between practitioners from different schools (*taryu-jiai*), became frowned upon by both the government and many of the ryuha themselves.[18]

One result of these developments was a rapid proliferation of new ryuha, spurred at least in part by the disappearing need for "masters" to prove their skills in public combat.[19] A second was a tendency for ryuha to become introverted in their training and outlook, since their kabala were no longer subject to continual polishing and refinement through exposure to the kabala of other schools.

Under such conditions, kata come to assume an enlarged role in the teaching and learning process. For new generations of first students and then teachers who had never known combat, pattern practice became their only exposure to martial skills. As instructors grew further and further away from battlefield and dueling experience, and as evaluation of student progress came to be based on performance in pattern practice alone, it became increasingly difficult to determine whether or not students actually understood the kata they were performing. In some schools, skill in pattern practice became an end in and of itself. Kata grew showier and more stylized, while trainees danced their way through them with little attempt to internalize anything but the outward form.

By the end of the seventeenth century, Ogyu Sorai and other self-styled experts on proper samurai behavior were already mourning the decline of the bugei and martial training. The warrior arts of ages past, they lamented, had degenerated into "flowery swordplay" (*kaho kenpo*) and gamesmanship. In the words of Fujita Toko, an early nineteenth century commentator,

> Tests of arms with live blades ceased to be conducted. When this happened, the various houses founded their own schools and practiced only within their own ryuha. Thus . . . [training] came to be like children's play wherein one studied only kata; the arts of sword and spear could not but decline.[20]

It should be emphasized, however, that the potential problems inherent in pattern practice are just that: *potential* problems, not *inevitable* ones. Not all ryuha lapsed into *kaho kenpo* during the middle Tokugawa period. Some were able to keep their kata alive, practical, and in touch with their roots, their kabala in the hands of men who had genuinely mastered it.[21] In this context Sorai seems to have drawn a distinction between the Toda-ryu and the Shinto-ryu, on the one hand, and the Yagyu Shinkage-ryu and the Itto-ryu, on the other.[22] Nevertheless, a good many ryuha gradually reified methods and conventions they did not fully understand and fossilized kata, passing on only the outward forms without fully comprehending the principles behind them.

This danger may have been particularly acute for schools such as the Yagyu Shinkage-ryu, in which the headship was restricted to a single family, as it was difficult to guarantee that each generation would produce a son equal to his ancestors in talent and diligence. In any event, by the end of the seventeenth century, the shortcomings of pattern practice were provoking both commentary and responses.

In the early 1700s, several sword schools in Edo began experimenting with protective gear to allow their students to spar with one another at full speed and power without injury.[23] This touched off a debate that continues to this day concerning the value and purpose of using such protective gear.

Proponents of sparring and the competitions that developed concomitantly argued that pattern practice alone cannot develop the seriousness of purpose, the courage, decisiveness, aggressiveness, and forbearance vital to true mastery of combat. Such skill can be fostered only by contesting with an equally serious opponent, not by dancing through kata. Pattern practice, moreover, forces students to pull their blows and slow them down, so they never develop speed and striking power. Competition, it was argued, is also needed to teach students how to read and respond to an opponent who is actually trying to strike them.

Kata purists, on the other hand, retorted that competitive sparring does not produce the same state of mind as real combat and is not, therefore, any more realistic a method of training than pattern practice. Sparring also inevitably requires rules and modifications of equipment that move trainees even further away from the conditions of duels and/or the battlefield. Moreover, sparring distracts students from the mastery of the kata and encourages them to develop their own moves and techniques before they have fully absorbed those of the ryuha.

The controversy persists today with little foreseeable prospect of resolution.[24] It is important for our purposes here to note that it represents a divergence in philosophy that transcends the label of traditionalists versus reformers sometimes applied to it. In the first place, the conflict is nearly three hundred years old, and the "traditionalist" position only antedates the "reformist" one by a few decades. In the second, advocates of sparring maintain that their methodology is actually closer to that employed in Sengoku and early Tokugawa times than is kata-only training. And in the third place, modem cognate martial arts schools—the true reformists—are divided over the issue, e.g., judo relies exclusively on sparring to evaluate students, while aikido tests only by means of kata, and kendo uses a combination of kata and sparring in its examinations.

In any event, one must be careful not to make too much of the quarrels surrounding pattern practice. For the disagreements are disputes of degree, not essence. All of the traditional ryuha that survive today utilize kata as their central form of training. None has abandoned it or subordinated it to other teaching techniques.

• • •

Kata, then, are a key component of traditional Japanese martial arts. They are kabala in motion, dynamic compendiums of the essential principles of the various schools. Pattern practice is the core of transmission in the traditional ryuha, the fundamental means for teaching and learning that body of knowledge that constitutes the school. Mastery of a ryuha's secrets is a suprarational process wherein one is first molded by, then freed from, and finally freed by the framework of the ryuha's kata.

NOTES

1. Western audiences usually equate kata training with the solo exercises of Chinese, Okinawan and Korean martial arts. But pattern practice in the Japanese bugei is fundamentally different from this sort of exercise. One important and obvious distinction is that kata in both traditional and modern Japanese fighting arts nearly always involve the participation of two or more people.
2. Fujiwara Yoshinobu, *Menhyoho no ki*, quoted in Nakabayashi Shinji, "Kenjutsu keiko no ikkosai," in *Budo ronko* (Ibaraki: Nakabayashi Shinji Sensei Isakushu Kangyokai, 1988), pp. 161-62. The publication date of this text is unknown, but it is believed to have been written in the late Edo period. The ryuha discussed is one from the Shinkage-ryu tradition, transmitted within the Nabeshima family.
3. cf. Tomiki Kenji, *Budo ron* (Tokyo: Daishukan Shoten, 1991), pp. 42-56, 60.
4. David Slawson, *Secret teachings in the art of Japanese gardens: Design principles and aesthetic values* (New York: Kodansha International, 1987), 54.
5. Fujiwara Yoshinobu, *Menhyoho no ki*, quoted in Nakabayashi Shinji, "Kenjutsu keiko no ikkosai," p. 165.
6. Issai Chozan, "Neko no myojutsu," reproduced in Watanabe Ichiro, ed., *Budo no meicho*, 15.
7. G. Victor Sogen Hori discusses at considerable length the notion of Development versus Self-Discovery (his terms), as it applies to Rinzai Zen Buddhist training in "Teaching and Learning in the Rinzai Zen Monastery," *Journal of Japanese Studies* 20:1 (1994), 25-32.
8. Fujiwara Yoshinobu, *Menhyoho no ki*, quoted in Nakabayashi Shinji, "Kenjutsu keiko no ikkosai," p. 166.
9. Hori, 11-2. The resemblance of bugei training to Zen practices has been noted by a number of observers. See, for example, D.T. Suzuki, *Zen and Japanese culture* (Princeton, NJ: Princeton University Press, 1959), 87-214; or Donn F. Draeger, *Classical budo* (New York: Weatherhill, 1973), 63-65.
10. Robert Eno, *The Confucian creation of heaven: Philosophy and the defense of ritual mastery* (Albany, NY: State University of New York Press, 1990), offers an insightful and provocative discussion of the meaning of ritual in early Confucianism. See especially, pp. 6-13 and 68-69.
11. For a general introduction to Neo-Confucianism, see Fung Yu-lan, *A short history of Chinese philosophy* (New York: The Free Press, 1948), 266-318.
12. Ronald Dore, *Education in Tokugawa Japan* (Berkeley, CA: University of California Press, 1965), 127.
13. Dore, 124-52.

[14] Hori, 5-7. Pattern practice and drill are also the key to the highly successful Kumon and Suzuki programs for teaching academic and musical skills in contemporary Japan. Nancy Ukai, "The kumon approach to teaching and learning," *Journal of Japanese Studies* 20:1 (1994), 87-113, is an enlightening discussion of the former.

[15] This concept is emphasized by many bugei ryuha in their choice of orthography for "kata." While most non-martial traditional Japanese arts, such as chanoyu, shoji, or ikebana, use one character, most bugei schools write it with a different character, with the explanation that the former implies a rigidity and constraint inappropriate to martial training. The latter, it is argued, better represents the freedom to respond and change—albeit within a pattern—essential to success in combat.

[16] Examples of such documents are reproduced in Imamura Yoshio, ed. *Nihon budo taike* (Tokyo: Dohosha Shuppan, 1982) v. 1, pp. 14, 20-21; v. 2, pp. 402-3, 439-62; v. 3, pp. 12-13; and Seki Hamitake, *Nihon budo no engen: Kashima-shinryu* (Tokyo: Kyorin Shoin, 1976), pp. 30-32.

[17] Ishioka Hisao, Wakada Kazuo, and Kato Hiroshi, *Nihon no kobujutsu* (Tokyo: Shinjinbutsu Oraisha, 1980), pp.15-18; Nakabayashi Shinji, "Kendo shi," in *Nihon budo taike* v. 10, pp. 40-42; Kurogi Toshiharu, "Budo ryuha no seiritsu to shugendo," *Saga-dai kyoiku gakubu kenkyu ronbunshu* 15 (1967), pp. 159-93. Tominaga Kengo, *Kendo gohykaunen-shi* (Tokyo: Hyakusen Shobo, 1971), 50-51 and 63-69, asserts that *musha shugyo* served a double purpose, helping a warrior to both hone his martial skills and attract the attention and interest of potential employers. Accounts of specific *musha shugyo* adventures can be found in Inagaki Moto, *Kengo no meishobu 100 wa* (Tokyo: Tatsukaze Shobo, 1982); Kobe Shinjuro, *Nihon kengodan* (Tokyo: Mainichi Shinbunsha, 1984); Okada Kazuo, *Kengo shidan* (Tokyo: Shinjinbutsu Oraisha, 1984); Watatani Kiyoshi, *Nihon kengo 100 en* (Tokyo: Akita Shoten, 1971); and Sugawara Makoto, *Lives of master swordsmen* (Tokyo: The East, 1985).

[18] The conventional wisdom among the Japanese authorities on this topic attributes the decline of *taryu-jiai* and *musha shugyo* to prohibition edicts issued in the mid-seventeenth century by the shogunate and quickly echoed by the lords of numerous domains and by many of the ryuha themselves (see, for example, Ishioka et al, *Nihon no kobujutsu*, p. 20; Nakabayashi, pp. 72-74; or Tominaga, pp. 272-75). A word of caution on this point is in order, however: the bans on taryu-jiai are mentioned by most studies on the subject, but we have been unable to identify the specific dates for the bans or to locate a primary source confirming them. Moreover, neither taryu-jiai nor *musha shugyo* disappeared completely as

the numerous accounts of celebrated duels during the middle and late Tokugawa period attest. In fact, Tominaga (p. 273) quotes two documents from the late seventeenth century, one issued by the government of Tsuyama domain in Mimasaka province and the other by a bugei school (the Asayama Ichiden-ryu), that both imply a general prohibition on taryu-jiai to have existed but also outline circumstances under which such contests were to be permitted. This is further evidence that duels and matches were still occurring, even if with restrictions.

[19] Although government prohibitions on inter-school contests did not eliminate the practice completely, they did provide a convenient excuse for any would-be instructor who wished to avoid such matches. A similar phenomenon appears to have occurred in the late twentieth century: The headmaster of one ryuha once commented to me that in the early 1960s, when taryu-jiai were common practice, there were only a handful of schools active in any public forum. Since the late 60s, when stricter Japanese government enforcement of its dueling laws put an end to taryu-jiai, the number of ryuha participating in demonstrations and the like has waxed appreciably (personal conversation with Dr. Seki Humitake, nineteenth-generation *shihanke*, Kashima-Shinryu, August 14, 1992).

[20] Quoted in Ishioka, et al, *Nihon no kobujutsu*, p. 20.

[21] This is attested to by the undefeated records, in dozens of taryu-jiai, of Kunni Zen'ya and Seki Humitake, two recent headmasters of the Kashima-Shinryu, a school which continues to train only through pattern practice.

[22] See the passage quoted in Ishioka et al, *Nihon no kobujutsu*, p. 21.

[23] Kamiizumi Ise no Kami Hidetsuna is believed to have been the first famous swordsman to adopt the bamboo practice sword (*fukuro shinai* or *hikihada*) in the late sixteenth century. Naganuma Shiro Saemon Kunisato, of the Jikishinkage-ryu, is usually credited with introducing head and wrist protection in the 1710s.

[24] For recent discussions of this issue, see Nakabayashi Shinji, "Kenjutsu keiko no ikkosai"; Yoshitani Osamu, "Kenjutsu kata no kozo to kin ni kansuru kenkyu," in Watanabe Ichiro kyoju taikan kinenkai, ed., *Nihon budogaku kenkyu* (Tokyo: Shimazu Shobo, 1988), pp. 114-29; Tomiki Kenji, *Budo ron* (Tokyo: Taishukan Shoten, 1991), pp. 5-9, 13-25, 52-101; or Iwai Tsukuo, *Kobujutsu tankyu* (Tokyo: Airyudo, 1991), pp. 58-67, 88-107.

REFERENCES

Dore, R. (1965). *Education in Tokugawa Japan*. Berkeley, CA: University of California Press.

Draeger, D. (1973). *Classical budo*. New York: Weatherhill.

Eno, R. (1990). *The Confucian creation of heaven: Philosophy and the defense of ritual mastery*. Albany, NY: State University of New York Press.

Fung, Y. L. (1948). *A short history of Chinese philosophy*. New York: The Free Press.

Hori, G. V. S. (1994). "Teaching and learning in the Rinzai Zen monastery," *Journal of Japanese Studies* 20 (1), 5-35.

Imamura, Y. (Ed). (1982). *Nihon budo taike 1-3*. Tokyo: Dohosha Shuppan.

Inagaki, M. (1982). *Kengo no meishobu 100 wa*. Tokyo: Tatsukaze Shobo.

Ishioka, H., Kazuo, W., and Hiroshi, K. (1980). *Nihon no kobujutsu*. Tokyo: Shinhin Butsu Oraisha.

Iwai, T. (1991). *Kobujutsu tankyu*. Tokyo: Airyudo.

Kobe, S. (1984). *Nihon kengodan*. Tokyo: Mainichi Shinbunsha.

Kurogi, T. (1967). "Budo ryuha no seiritsu to shugendo." *Saga-dai kyoiku gakubu kenkyu ronbunshu* 15, 159-193.

Nakabayashi, S. (1982). "Kendo shi," in *Nihon budo taikei* 10, 29-113.

Nakabayashi, S. (1988). "Kenjutsu keiko no ikkosai," in *Budo ronko* (Ibaraki: Nakabayashi Shinji Sensi Isakushu Kangyokai), 160-168.

Okada, K. (1984). *Kengo shidan*. Tokyo: Shinjinbutsu Oraisha.

Seki, H. (1976). *Nihon budo no engen: Kashimu-shinryu*. Tokyo: Kyorin Shoin.

Slawson, D. (1987). *Secret teachings in the art of Japanese gardens: Design principles and aesthetic values*. New York: Kodansha International.

Sugawara, M. (1985). *Lives of master swordsmen*. Tokyo: The East.

Suzuki, D. T. (1959). *Zen and Japanese culture*. Princeton, NJ: Princeton University Press.

Tomiki, K. (1991). *Budo ron*. Tokyo: Daishukan shoten.

Tominaga, K. (1971). *Kendo gohykaunen-shi*. Tokyo: Hyakusen shobo.

Ukai, N. (1994). "The kumon approach to teaching and learning," *Journal of Japanese Studies* 20, 1.

Watanabe, I. (Ed). (1979). *Budo no meicho*. Tokyo: Tokyo Kopii Shuppanbu.

Watanabe, K. (1971). *Nihon kengo 100 en*. Tokyo: Akita Shoten.

Yoshitani, O. (1988). "Kenjutsu kata no kozo to kin ni kansuru kenkyu." In Watanabe Ichiro kyoju taikan kinenkai, (Ed.), *Nihon budogaku kenkyu* (Tokyo: Shimazu Shobo), 114-29.

chapter 7

IDEAL TEACHING: JAPANESE CULTURE AND THE TRAINING OF THE WARRIOR

by Wayne W. Van Horne, Ph.D.

Wa, the principle of "group harmony, is demonstrated through the synchronized movements of students practicing a kata in Shorinji-ryu Karatedo. *Photos courtesy of W. Van Horne.*

The central themes of Japanese culture have evolved over the past several centuries and permeate all aspects of life in Japan, including martial arts (Befu, 1971: 174-179; Beasley, 1975: 11-13). Perhaps the most central theme is the strong emphasis on conformity and the subordinating of individualism to the norms of the social group (Befu, 1971: 168-169). Yet, one prominent image in Japanese culture seems to conspicuously contrast with this emphasis on conformity—the idealized image of the lone samurai warrior.

Many of us are familiar with the idealized image of the lone warrior as depicted in the famous Akira Kurasawa/Toshiro Mifune samurai films such as "The Seven Samurai." The lone warrior of these films is an independent individualist, who is an ultimately competent, invincible, and technically superb warrior, who single-handedly triumphs in combat against the multitudes of adversaries who oppose him. Is this seeming anomaly of the heroic individualist in a culture of conformity based on our erroneous Western interpretation of the Japanese warrior image, or is the individualism of the warrior actually prized in modern conformity-ridden Japanese culture?

One way to answer this question is to examine the relationship between the teaching methods of Japanese martial arts systems, the training ground of warriors, and key Japanese cultural values. Do the training methods teach individualism, or are they consistent with the cultural value of conformity?

My research indicates that although the teaching methods do indeed train martial artists to be highly skilled individual fighters who engage in one-on-one combat, the ultimate goal of the training is consistent with broader Japanese cultural values—to create individuals who contribute to the betterment of the collective society and who have a high degree of social responsibility—a conclusion that has also been drawn by other researchers (Befu, 1971: 166-169; Jones, 1992).[1]

The comparative analysis of martial arts training methods that I am presenting is based on data I obtained through participant observation and interviews as a student in three different systems of Japanese *budo*, or martial arts. In each of these arts—Sakugawa Koshiki Shorinji-ryu Karatedo, Aikido of Ueshiba, and Shinto Muso-ryu Jodo—the teachers I observed were highly ranked, had been trained through traditional Japanese methods, and likewise, train their students with traditional methods.[2] Two of the teachers are Japanese, and one is an American who learned his art in Japan.

The teaching methods and goals of all of these systems are strikingly similar, so much so that it is obvious that they are widely used, culturally based methods of teaching that embody Japanese cultural ideals. Their overt goal is to mold a student toward a specific end, the creation of a master *budoka*, a warrior who embodies not only supreme competence in the specific martial art, but also embodies many of the ideals of Japanese culture (cf. Jones, 1992).

In order to examine the relationship between Japanese culture, teaching methods in the martial arts, and the ultimate goals of warrior training, I will discuss several major Japanese cultural themes that serve as models for teaching methods in the martial arts. I will also use examples from my participant observation to illustrate the influence that these cultural themes have on actual martial arts teaching and goals.

Theme One: Conformity (*Wa, Masubi, Giri,* and *Ninjo*)

The first major theme is one of the most pervasive themes in Japanese culture—the importance of social conformity and the subordinating of individual desires to the needs of the group. This ethos of group conformity provides the model for the structure of group training in budo. Several uniquely Japanese concepts relate to this theme, specifically *wa*, *musubi*, *giri*, and *ninjo*.

Wa is the concept of group harmony, the subordinating of the individual to the collective functioning of the group (Whiting, 1979). *Wa* serves as a cultural model for group martial arts practice. For example, in karatedo, jodo, and aikido classes, students practice basic techniques (*kihon waza*) repetitively as a group. Students are required to achieve a remarkable degree of synchronization and uniformity in their collective movements, most strikingly seen in the group practice of elaborate *kata*, or patterns of techniques, in karatedo. Students are taught to act in harmony with the group, not to perform as individuals. Those who do act as individuals cannot move in synchronization with the rest of the group and are admonished by teachers for disrupting the group *wa*. In a perfect kata performed by a class of students, everyone moves not as individuals, but as a group entity, each individual a part of the collective *wa*.

Musubi, a related concept which means unity or harmonious interaction, is central to aikido theory. *Musubi* extends the ideal of group harmony to harmony with the attacker. Aikido students typically train in pairs, with one student attacking and one defending. Aikido technique is based on the defender blending with, or coming into harmony with, the motion and energy of the attacker—in other words applying *musubi* (Saotome, 1989: 9).

Giri is another core cultural concept that refers to the individual's social obligation or duty to act appropriately while interacting with others—in other words, to conform to appropriate cultural rules of social interaction (Nitobe, 1979: 24-25; Befu, 1971: 168-169). Individuals must, therefore, suppress their personal, natural inclinations and desires, their individualistic tendencies, known as *ninjo* (Befu, 1971: 169-170). This conformity to appropriateness of behavior also extends to the ideal of "correctness," the ideal that there are specific, correct ways of doing things. In Japanese culture, especially where ritual is used, the Japanese believe there is an optimally correct way for actions to be performed that can only be learned through exact imitation of a master of the art or ritual. There is, therefore, a high value placed on conformity with the approved method of doing something. For example, this can be seen in instructional methods used in the educational system and in arts such as Noh and the tea ceremony.

Students who practice budo are also admonished to imitate the techniques of their teachers exactly, without individual variation or expression, in order to master the technique correctly. In all of the arts I observed, the major emphasis was to drill students repetitively in individual techniques and combinations of techniques to enable them to perform with painstaking precision. In jodo, for example, students were required to spend hours mastering each individual basic strike with a staff (*jo*) before beginning to learn combinations of techniques. The first several classes typically consist of practicing a strike over and over again for two or three hours, with the teacher correcting it until the student can do it precisely. My karatedo teacher often made this same point by telling students that as beginners they were like puppets, their goal being to imitate their teacher as precisely as possible. Another American aikido teacher I observed made this point by telling students that the process of learning aikido was similar to that of art. Students had to learn to draw basic shapes, such as squares, circles, etc., precisely before they would ultimately be able to create a painting of complex form.

Precision in performing techniques is emphasized in budo training. Here seventh-dan Thomas Cauley, International Director of Sakugawa Shorinji-ryu Karatedo, demonstrates the correct technique in a sai kata. *Photo courtesy of W. Van Horne.*

The emphasis on conformity to the group and conformity in execution of techniques has multiple goals in Japanese training methods. Technical mastery is certainly foremost. Learning the techniques precisely ultimately allows the budoka to perform their techniques in the quickest, most powerful, and most efficacious manner possible and optimizes their ability to survive a fight. It also builds endurance, physical stamina, and strength. However, it also allows the teacher to observe and assess the personality of each student. The student's patience, natural aptitude, commitment, and to perseverance—all essential qualities to train and survive as a warrior—become apparent. Teachers look for weaknesses in these abilities and give individualized instruction to their students to point out their weaknesses and force them to improve. Throughout this process, apt students learn about their own character and personality and attempt to overcome their weaknesses. My karatedo teacher addressed this issue by saying that a *shodan*, or first-degree black belt, was only considered a beginner. All of the training prior to that merely allowed a student to learn some basics but more importantly allowed the teacher to assess the student's character. The most important training began after a student proved he had the qualities necessary to become a warrior.

This teaching method is also apparent in jodo training. New students are required to master each basic technique one at a time. This means that new students must practice the same technique repetitively for hours during a class, often practicing by themselves. Of course, many new students become bored and don't see the purpose of the tedious repetition. The jodo teacher would observe the way that new students dealt with the repetitive solo practice and would comment about weaknesses he perceived, such as not having patience, not concentrating, etc. In this respect, the initial, tedious basic practice serves as a sort of litmus test for gauging the personalities of new students. Many new students don't persevere through this initial phase.

Theme Two: Hierarchy (*On* and *Amae*)

The second major theme that pervades budo training is derived from the importance of hierarchy as a model for the structure of Japanese society (Beasley, 1975: 3-4). Two concepts are particularly important in order to understand the effects of hierarchy in Japanese culture and behavior (Befu, 1971: 31-32, 54, 166-168; Benedict, 1974: 98-113). The first is *amae*, the tendency to depend on the approval or love of other significant people in one's life for one's own emotional happiness (Befu, 1971: 159-161). The other, *on*, refers to indebtedness that can never be repaid. For instance, a child can never repay its parents for its birth and their love and effort to raise it. Likewise, a student can never repay a teacher for his knowledge and teaching, or an employee a boss for his hiring and employment. The best one can do is to fulfill to the best of one's ability any obligations to, or requests from, those people. These are examples of *on*.

On also functions between student and teacher in budo training. Students have strong obligations and bonds to their teachers, to the extent that traditionally teachers were supported, and cared for, by their students. The cultural importance of *on*, indebtedness, and *giri*, appropriateness, are such that together they create a strong sense of obligation in students to do whatever the teacher asks (Nitobe, 1979: 37-41). Budo teachers are in a position of hierarchical status and authority over students, and they use their students' sense of indebtedness and need for approval to make ever-increasing demands for training time and acquisition of skills. They also use the students' sense of *on* to manipulate and motivate them during training.

This was most apparent to me in jodo training. Increasing demands were placed on students as they gained more seniority in the class. For example, students were typically shown a kata, or prearranged series of techniques, only once or twice by the teacher, and then were expected to know it by the next practice. Newer students would usually forget the kata. The teacher would seem to become very angry with the students and would tell them that since they had forgotten the kata they had wasted his time in teaching it to them. The horror of this to Japanese students is that they have both failed in their obligation to a person of higher status, someone to whom they are indebted, and have met with disapproval from a significant person in their life. They would then typically work extremely hard to learn what was required of them and not make this mistake again.

The students' sense of obligation also motivates them to tolerate a variety of severe teaching methods. In jodo, the teacher would often use anger to teach a variety of lessons—to show disapproval of failure to learn, to motivate students to learn faster, or to teach them to deal with their temper or a stressful situation. He would also use disapproval to the same end, sometimes walking away from a student in the middle of private instruction in apparent disgust, leaving the student confused and alone in the middle of the practice floor in front of the class. I also observed the aikido teacher become angry and threaten to walk out in the middle of a large seminar he was conducting with a hundred or so students—because they weren't performing a technique exactly the way he had showed it. The threat had the desired effect and motivated the students to perform the technique exactly as demonstrated. In each of these examples, the teacher used anger and disapproval to manipulate the students' sense of *on* and *amae* in order to motivate them to learn.

The students' sense of *on* also motivates them to endure teaching methods involving physical pain. For example, once the jodo teacher was reviewing with me a particularly long and complicated kata that I had failed to master. It entailed my attacking him with a wooden practice sword (*tachi*) and his defending with a short wooden staff (*jo*). Over a number of repetitions, he continuously increased the intensity, speed, and power of his techniques to make the situation more and more like actual combat. He interjected angry comments and looks of disgust at my incompetence throughout this process. This culminated in a very real, though expertly controlled, attack by him on the last repetition of the kata that resulted in my sustaining a split lip, a nearly broken arm, and a bruising blow to my solar plexus that caused me a momentary blackout and a wave of intense nausea. Needless to say, the reality and danger he instilled in the situation resulted in an increase in the intensity and skill of my practice from then on.

A similar experience occurred at a comparable level of my karatedo training. Over the course of an hour, my teacher repeatedly told me to punch at him and repeatedly threw me over his shoulder onto a wooden gymnasium floor with a series of impressive techniques. The pain and exhaustion I experienced from attacking and being thrown resulted in my attacking him as hard as I possibly could with every ounce of energy I had left in order to just keep going. Eventually, I ceased to give any thought to the consequences of my attacks. When he halted this practice, he told me that I had finally learned to perform a committed attack, which was necessary in order for my techniques to actually work in combat. I then realized that this had been his goal and was the lesson I was supposed to learn.

Japanese students endure many physically grueling lessons like these, and return to practice again due to their sense of *on* to their teacher. Again, teachers have multiple goals when utilizing a student's sense of *on* and *awe*. The students' sense of obligation and desire for approval motivates intense practice, which is characterized by the emphasis on the perfecting of techniques and consequently results in the attainment of a high level of mastery of technical skills (Befu, 1971: 174). It also allows students to develop courage and calmness in the face of unpredictable, intense lessons in the dojo. The goal is ultimately pragmatic—the few students who endure to the culmination of this process become master warriors, better than the vast majority of fighters (Nitobe, 1979: 28-29).

Theme Three: Universal Law (*Ri* and *Ji*)

A third major theme in Japanese culture, more focused in the areas of religion, spiritual beliefs, and the arts, is the belief that universal natural laws exist and can be manifested through the actions of a master of an art. Two concepts associated with this ideal are *ri* and *ji*. *Ri* is universal truth, the following of universal laws of nature, while *ji* is a particular action or expression of *ri* created by a master. In essence, *ji* is a depiction or manifestation of the universal truth, which can only be produced by someone with the insight to produce it. In budo, a technique or kata performed by a master is *ji*—it is perfect and follows the natural laws (Leggett, 1978: 122-126). In order to master an art to the level that a budoka can express *ji* in his actions, every technique must be mastered, the principles of biomechanics and *ki* (energy) flow must be understood, calmness of mind in combat and invincibility of spirit must be mastered, the universal principles must be applied to all action, and all of these must be integrated within the budoka. With this high level of mastery, a budoka becomes not only a master fighter, but his actions become *ji* and manifest the universal truths.

Saotome, a disciple of the founder of aikido, discusses this through a related concept of *kannagara*:

> *Kannagara* is a way of intuition. . . . The only laws are the laws which govern natural phenomena and promote harmony. *Kannagara* is a way of supreme freedom, for the action appropriate to function in harmony with nature occurs spontaneously.
>
> –Jones, 1982: 124

A goal in aikido practice is to spontaneously apply technique.
Photo courtesy of W. Van Horne.

Saotome's words explicate the Japanese cultural model of mastery of an art—it is only after mastering the art that the warrior can truly become creative and spontaneous. The spontaneity will then be in harmony with the universal laws of nature, and the warrior will be invincible. Thus, the emphasis in teaching methods on precise imitation, repetition, and technical mastery. It is only with this level of exacting training that mastery can be achieved. For example, my jodo teacher would sometimes quip, "When you have a *menkyo kaiden* [or have mastered the system], you can perform this technique the way that you want, but for now we do it the way our headmaster teaches us." The point that this makes is that a student needs to imitate the teacher to reach the level of mastery and insight necessary to perform a perfect technique spontaneously.

Again, the ultimate goal of this training model is pragmatic for the warrior who faces combat and death. My jodo teacher told me that the ultimate goal of budo is to train hard to become as good as possible as quickly as possible, so that one will be able to defeat an opponent with one's spirit. His point is that, if you are a master, then your capabilities will be so apparent in your attitude and actions that any opponent will recognize that he will be defeated and, therefore, won't attack. This is perceived as the ultimate pragmatic goal of budo training—a warrior becomes invincible in art and spirit, and, therefore, violence is averted.

Theme Four: Enlightenment and Transcendence

The last theme, which is again more specific to spirituality and the arts, is that of enlightenment and transcendence through mastery (Suzuki, 1973). This is the ultimate goal of budo training. The training not only produces master warriors, but leads to the realization in the master budoka that he does not want to kill. Again, teaching methods are used to instill this lesson from the beginning.

My karatedo teacher once had an aggressive new student join his class specifically for the purpose of sparring with other students. The teacher asked him to spar with him before class, and the new student eagerly accepted. The teacher had no difficulty in repeatedly inflicting painful, although controlled techniques on him. Within five minutes the student was bruised and bloodied. He then proceeded to practice with the rest of the class for two hours.

This process of enduring painful sparring before class with the teacher was repeated at the beginning of each class for almost a month. The student became at first more determined to fight hard, then gradually became resigned to the fighting, and eventually realized that not only was fighting self-destructive, but that he no longer wished to inflict such pain on other students. Finally, when it was apparent that he was no longer interested in fighting, the teacher ceased to fight him in this manner. I must add that whenever the teacher sparred with other students he did not hurt them. When asked about his purpose in the brutal treatment of the student, the teacher answered that "some people need to be shown love the hard way."

A similar incident occurred with the jodo teacher. One new student who was aggressive in his practice with other students suffered repeated lectures and bursts of apparent anger from the teacher. Again, the teacher attempted to teach him that budo training was not about aggression. The ultimate goal of budo training is to transcend violence and anger, again for multiple reasons.

Pragmatically, a warrior who has emotional control during battle has a better chance of surviving. A warrior who is angry or violent is not in harmony with universal laws and will be defeated. More importantly, by becoming a master budoka a warrior is invincible, and, therefore, doesn't need to kill another human. With this ability comes the realization that killing is unnecessary. A master budoka with this realization is motivated to train others to this level of mastery so that they too avert conflict. The outcome of budo training is, therefore, the instilling of benevolence in the budoka as well as a sense of social responsibility to teach others for the betterment of society.

Conclusion

The teaching methods that I have described budo teachers using are obviously derived from important Japanese cultural themes such as conformity, the importance of the group, correctness, indebtedness, harmony with nature, and transcendence. They are indeed focused on the pragmatic goal of developing a superb fighter, but this is seen as necessary for the ultimate goal of creating insight which leads to the development of a personal ethos of benevolence and social responsibility.

This brings us back to the question I posed at the beginning: Is it the individualism of the warrior that is actually prized in modern conformity-ridden Japanese culture, or is this an erroneous interpretation of the idealized warrior image by Westerners? The answer at this point is apparent: the ideal of the budoka is that of an invincible warrior who is able to overcome all adversaries, but who ultimately embodies a deep sense of social obligation and is strongly motivated to better society by training others to be able to avoid violence through their own mastery of budo. The warrior image, therefore, embodies the cultural ideal of the individual's obligation to put society's needs above his own. Like the hero at the end of *Sanjuro* and other Kurasawa Mifune films, the master warrior in Japanese culture ultimately shuns violence and killing as personal weakness and social evil.

ACKNOWLEDGEMENTS

This paper is a result of the outstanding training I have received from the following teachers: Thomas Cauley, David E. Jones, David Adams, Norio Wada, Mitsugi Saotome, and Edward Baker. I thank them all for their efforts.

NOTES

[1] The conclusions presented in this paper are my own and do not necessarily reflect the opinions of any of the martial arts teachers whom I observed during my fieldwork.

[2] My participant observation consisted of five years direct training with Thomas Cauley, *shichidan* (seventh-degree black belt) in Sakugawa Koshiki Shorinji-ryu Karatedo, two years with Norio Wada, *godan* (fifth-degree black belt) in Shinto Muso-ryu Jodo, and attendance over a twelve-year period at numerous seminars taught by Mitsugi Saotome, *shihan* (master teacher) of Aikido of Ueshiba.

BIBLIOGRAPHY

Beasley, W. G. (1975). *The modern history of Japan.* New York: Praeger.

Befu, H. (1971). *Japan: An anthropological introduction.* New York: Harper and Row.

Benedict, R. (1974). *The chrysanthemum and the sword.* New York: The New American Library.

Jones, D. (1992). Testing for shodan in Japan: Kyudo and jodo. *Journal of Asian Martial Arts, 1* (1), 68-71.

Jones, D. (1982) Saotome: Twentieth century samurai. *Phoenix Journal of Transpersonal Anthropology,* VI, (1-2), 116-131.

Leggett, T. (1978). *Zen and the ways.* Boulder, CO: Shambhala.

Nitobe, I. (1979). *Bushido: The warriors code.* Burbank, CA: Ohara.

Saotome, M. (1989). *The principles of aikido.* Boston, MA: Shambhala.

Suzuki, D. T. (1973). *Zen and Japanese culture.* Princeton, NJ: Princeton University Press.

Turnbull, S. (1982). *The book of the samurai.* New York: W. H. Smith.

Whiting, R. (Sept., 1979). "You've gotta have 'wa.'" *Sports Illustrated,* pp. 60-61.

chapter 8

MODERN EDUCATIONAL THEORIES AND TRADITIONAL JAPANESE MARTIAL ARTS TRAINING METHODS

by John J. Donohue, Ph.D.

All illustrations are from the graphic novel series by
Oscar Ratti and Adele Westbrook: *Tales of the Hermit*.
Illustrations by O. Ratti.
© 2001 & 2004 Futuro Designs and Publications.

Introduction: The Way of the Ways

Students of many modern Japanese martial arts are fond of reminding us that, as the Japanese term *budo* implies, they are really "martial ways." The destination of these ways is varied: they can be understood as systems of physical exercise or spiritual development, as relatively efficient physiological (as opposed to technological) systems, as recreational and competitive sports or as civilian self-defense methods. In fact, any intense scrutiny of these systems reveals a multifaceted nature, in which aspects of all these things can be recognized. The deeper the understanding of *budo*, the greater their recognized complexity.

This sophistication relates not merely to the techniques and systems themselves, but, I maintain, to the way in which they have been taught within the Japanese martial tradition. This represents another avenue of scientific inquiry for researchers focusing on sociological interpretations of martial arts activity. To date, work has explored topics such as the historical development and organizational structure of martial arts organizations within Asia in general (Draeger and Smith, 1989; Ratti and Westbrook, 1973), in Japan, and beyond (Hurst, 1998; Donohue, 1991, 1994). Research by a number of scholars has established some fairly well-defined and consistent organizational characteristics within traditional modern Japanese martial and other art forms (Hsu, 1975; O'Neill, 1984). Commentary has, to date, focused on the role of organizational paradigms in perpetuating elements of traditional culture, of promoting individual and group identity, and fostering the spread of ideologies associated with Asian culture. What is often overlooked is the pedagogical rationale embedded in the organization of modern martial arts forms. At a very basic level, they are organizations devoted to the transmission of skills and insights. As such, they have an overtly educational function. This chapter, based upon secondary sources and primary research in modern budo conducted over more than two decades, analyzes the organizational components of traditional martial arts training and relates them to modern pedagogical theories. It concludes that the instructional theory embedded in martial arts training is at least as sophisticated and highly developed as are the techniques and philosophies of these systems.

Japanese Martial Art Systems: Bugei, Bujutsu and Budo

We should first make clear that the current discussion focuses on the more widespread, "mass market" martial systems imported to the West from Japan. While the more expansive term *bugei* can be used for all extant martial arts forms, I make most explicit reference to those referred to as *budo* (martial ways) or *shin budo* (new martial ways). They are a distinct category of activities in the Japanese martial arts continuum.

These arts are essentially modern, cognate systems that tend, in general, to have been formulated in the late 19th and early 20th centuries. While technical, philosophical and esthetic factors can be demonstrated as being rooted in older systems, these modern budo forms were developed for practice by civilian populations. For this reason, considerable technical modification took place in the interest of making the arts both safer for practitioners and more tolerable to governmental authorities.

A few illustrative examples should suffice. The unarmed system of grappling called Kodokan Judo was developed in 1882 by Kano Jigoro. It had its basis in a variety of older systems of jujutsu, which enjoyed considerable popularity as unarmed fighting methods in urban Japan at the time. Kano combined the throwing, choking, wrestling, and striking techniques of various jujutsu systems into what he felt was a more "rational" and scientific curriculum. At the same time, Kano had high hopes that the system he devised, called *judo* to emphasize its more wholesome ethical character, would come to be widely practiced by the Japanese. To facilitate this spread, he modified techniques to eliminate some of the more damaging attacks, specified a training uniform with reinforced collar that could be used to hold a training partner and control a fall, created a systematic type of instruction that included the invaluable art of falling down, and devised a system of coded belt colors that permitted judo practitioners to be immediately classified as to the level of relative skill (Kano, 1986).

Kendo is another example of *shin budo* that reflects a modification of technique in the interest of safety and popular practice. Although popularly understood as the art of Japanese fencing, kendo is not the same art that was practiced by the feudal swordsmen of Japan, the bushi or samurai. It is a modern system which developed out of the arts of these feudal warriors, but it is very different. Kendo has rules, combat does not. The restriction of kendo blows to eight areas has made a noticeable change in kendo *bogu* (armor) when compared to the war armor of the samurai. The *shinai*, the bamboo foil utilized in kendo, is used differently from a real sword, is shaped and balanced differently from the katana, and is (a most important consideration) not a lethal weapon. Kendo's stance and movements have been conditioned by the fact that *kendoka* (kendo practitioners) typically train indoors on a hardwood floor. Feudal warriors fought on battlefields. These are a few examples of technical considerations that have decisively effected the evolution of technique and equipment in kendo (Sasamori and Warner, 1964; Donohue, 1999).

In addition to making training safer, the modifications commonly found in modern budo forms also render them appropriate for sportive and competitive interpretations. While not the case for all budo forms (such as iaido and aikido) sport competition in arts like karatedo, judo, and kendo have become central vehicles for these arts, and are one of the main motivators for participation by many people.

When presented as modern, ritualized, syncretic activities, it becomes quite clear that what are commonly referred to as "martial arts" are really "martially inspired arts" with little or no realistic combat utility in the modern world. Here we enter the extremely problematic area of labels. The Japanese themselves refer to what Westerners call martial arts with a variety of terms: *bugei* (the most expansive and literal term), *heiho* or *hyoho*, *bujutsu* (often reserved for more traditional forms of combat), *budo* (martial ways) and even the archaic *kyuba no michi* (the way of horse and bow). For some, the terms are used with a conscious precision that stresses some important aspect of the arts under discussion. This specificity is normally absent in popular discussions of these phenomena.

In the West, the seminal work by Donn Draeger (1973a, 1973b, 1974) established a terminological distinction between *bujutsu* (martial systems) and *budo* (martial ways). He suggested reserving *bujutsu* for references to the overtly military combat systems of the samurai and using *budo* to signify the modern cognate forms designed to appeal to civilians by virtue of their esthetic and sportive emphases. Popularly, Draeger's dichotomy has been interpreted as creating a distinction between overtly functional fighting systems on the one hand and philosophical vehicles on the other. This is correct in some aspects; bujutsu place a strong emphasis on combat utility, while many modern budo present training as a vehicle for character building and personal development and have little or no real fighting utility—but there is a certain lack of precision in erroneously presenting bujutsu as arts with no intellectual or philosophical sophistication (Friday, 1997: 163).

Draeger himself was certainly aware of the intellectual sophistication of bujutsu through his association with the Tenshin Katori Shinto-ryu. At the same time, faced with an erroneous popular conception that the modern budo forms were real fighting arts of the samurai, he felt that the distinction between combat oriented and civilian oriented arts was important enough to be stressed through the bujutsu/budo contrast. I agree.

Since the widespread popular usage of the term "martial arts" includes budo forms, this terminology is used in general terms in this chapter. When referring to "martial arts," I will be including both bujutsu and budo. When contrasting traditional/combat arts with modern/cognate forms, I will use the bujutsu/budo contrast.

CHARACTERISTICS OF MARTIAL ARTS SYSTEMS

Corporate Entities

In sociological terms, we can understand Japanese martial arts as corporate entities with a strongly hierarchical organization and an explicit ideological charter. These structural factors condition the process of training to a great degree and so bear some further discussion.

In the first place, Japanese martial arts seem to share a predilection for formal organization that can be contrasted to the approach in other Asian countries. From the Tokugawa Period (1603-1868) onward we note a marked tendency for martial arts training to be organized in corporate entities (Hurst, 1990). Schools came to have both a physical location, the *dojo* (literally "way place," the training hall) as well as a formal identity. Traditional bujutsu systems were often referred to as *ryu* (literally "streams," which gives some sense of the idea of corporate perpetuation), thus the Ono-ha Itto-ryu, the Yagyu Shinkage-ryu, etc. Usage in budo forms is a bit more varied: some systems maintain the ryu label, others use the more modern designation of *kan* (hall) such as in Kodokan Judo or Shotokan Karatedo (Funakoshi, 1973), or *kai* (association) as in Kyokushinkai Karatedo (Oyama, 1973).

Hierarchical Organizations

These organizations are hierarchical entities, in which issues of rank (related to skill and seniority) condition behavior. At the pinnacle of the organization is the *sensei*, or teacher, who is contrasted with his *montei*, or disciples. In addition to this gross distinction, there are finer gradations present as well. Students are enmeshed in a dualistic series of relationships between superiors and subordinates that are modeled on the teacher/student split and which echo general structural principles in Japanese society (Nakane, 1970). Thus, a series of relativistic links between *sempai* (seniors) and *kyohai* (juniors) also shapes behavior in the dojo (Donohue, 1991b).

The stratified nature of martial arts organizations is reinforced through the well-known ranking systems contained within them. Awareness of rank in these organizations is often buttressed by elaborate symbolic means such as methods of address and ritual bowing. In some systems, elements of training uniforms or their color are used to denote status. In some aikido schools only trainees above a specific level are permitted to wear the *hakama*, a pleated split skirt common to many bujutsu and budo systems. Among students in the Kashima Shin-ryu, the color of the hakama can indicate rank. The most well-known item of clothing associated with rank is the colored belt system adopted in many modern budo forms. In this system, trainees are classified according to *kyu* (class) and *dan* (grade). While permutations in hue and numbering are almost as varied as schools themselves, beginners in *kyu* levels usually wear white belts and, as they progress in rank, are awarded a series of different colored belts, culminating in the black belt, a sign that the trainee has reached dan level.

Modern budo grading systems are different from those of more traditional bujutsu systems extant today, as well as from feudal systems. For professional warriors of the past, elaborate grading systems were unnecessary, since survival was the most reliable indicator of combat proficiency.

As they are organized today, budo organizations share a commonality with a widespread organizational type in Japan, the *iemoto* (Hsu, 1975). Although most martial arts organizations are not formally identified by the Japanese as iemoto proper, they possess the highly structured hierarchical organization based on personal links between masters and disciples that are commonly the central characteristics of *iemoto* organization.

Iemoto are typically associated with the teaching and licensing of various art forms. By virtue of master/disciple links, the head of an iemoto can regulate a vast pyramidal organization with numerous branches in various locations. For martial arts systems, iemoto-like structure would only have been possible after the feudal era. Until that time, the prospect of warriors with allegiance to an organization that transcended local political boundaries would have been intolerable (Hurst, 1995).

Today, the iemoto-like structure of many martial arts forms can be understood as the offspring of general hierarchical characteristics in Japanese society (Nakane, 1970) as well as the demands of a market economy. In an effort to ensure "product quality," centralized control of systems ensures standardization of technique, ranking systems, and licensing. Coordination of outreach and the allocation of teaching territories by a central organization both have beneficial economic functions. In addition, control of an art by a formal organization serves to make these groups more easily policed and controlled, and hence, more politically palatable. This is certainly the case, for instance, when we review the process of development in Japanese budo organizations after the post-war ban on martial arts practice in Japan from 1945-48.

An Ideological Charter

As formal organizations, budo systems also have an explicit ideological charter—a mission statement in the corporate jargon of our times. These charters certainly relate to the philosophical orientation of many Japanese martial arts forms (whether of the *jutsu* or *do* variety). Broadly speaking, many martial arts, and particularly budo systems, are inspired by a mix of Shinto, Confucian and Buddhist ideas that link training with a type of personal/spiritual development. Much has been made, of course, of the alleged link between Zen and the martial arts (Suzuki, 1960; King, 1993; Leggett, 1978). While it is certainly possible that this connection was important for selected martial artists, it is neither universal nor historically accurate. Ueshiba Morihei, founder of aikido, is a good example of a martial arts master who was vastly more influenced by the precepts of Shinto than by Zen (Stevens, 1987).

In fact, while not for a moment calling into question the sincerity of modern martial artists, an objective assessment of martial arts charters reveal them to be vaguely formulated statements that present these arts as ways to advance the technical practice of the art in question, to celebrate human potential, and to advance causes as diffuse and universally unobjectionable as good sportsmanship and world peace. Even in the case of the formulation of some relatively specific ideological goals, as seems to be the case in aikido, continued organizational growth seems to bring with it a watering down of specific elements (Donohue, 1997) to make the philosophy palatable to a wide variety of practitioners. These ideas, in short, are made broadly acceptable and politically "safe." The charter of the All-Japan Kendo Federation is fairly characteristic:

> The concept of Kendo is to discipline the human character
> through the application of the principles of the katana.
> The purpose of practicing Kendo is:
> To mold the mind and body,
> To cultivate a vigorous spirit,
> And through correct and rigid training,
> To strive for improvement in the art of Kendo;
> To hold in esteem human courtesy and honor,
> To associate with others with sincerity,
> And to forever pursue the cultivation of oneself.
> Thus will one be able to love his country and society, to
> contribute to the development of culture, and to promote
> peace and prosperity among all peoples.
> —quoted in Donohue, 1999: 32

Charters of this type are useful in that they provide an overarching philosophical rationale (however diffuse) for what would otherwise be merely highly stylized calisthenics. In addition, these charters can be understood as the direct consequence of two things: the need to "rehabilitate" the martial arts after the Second World War and a related attempt to homogenize elements of indigenous Japanese ideology so as to be more easily accepted as these arts spread to the West. It is interesting that this diffuse mysticism has had an unexpected appeal for Westerners seeking alternatives to traditional Western belief systems.

EDUCATIONAL COMPONENTS

The martial arts organizations we are examining are like the techniques contained within them: rooted in the feudal past, but with concrete connections to Tokugawa (1603-1868) and modern era Japan. Until this time, martial training was rather ad hoc in terms of its organization and process, reflecting the vagaries of circumstance and individual instructor preference. It was only with the unification of the Tokugawa government that we begin to see a systemization of instruction in both *bun* and *bu*—the ways of civilian administration and military science (Dore, 1965).

Curricula

Although there is substantial variation in the techniques and purposes of various bujutsu and budo systems, there is a relative uniformity in terms of the shape of their curricula as they have emerged after the Tokugawa era. While specialized content may vary from art to art, there is general consistency in terms of how the knowledge set is organized and presented, especially within budo forms.

All these arts place a stress on fundamental elements. Such basics include a consideration of basic elements such as stance (which is conditioned by the art's objectives and the weapons employed), *ma-ai* (distance), timing, breathing (there is a well developed Asian emphasis on breath control in physical activities as well as meditation), as well as proper body management (*taisabaki*).

The *waza*, or techniques of a particular art, are built on this foundation. While armed or unarmed combat is, in reality, a fast moving flow of action, the building blocks of strike, parry, evasion, throw, etc. are isolated in the practice of waza. These basic techniques are relentlessly practiced and assiduously pursued as the key to ultimate mastery.

When a trainee has progressed to the point where the fundamentals can be combined with confidence, kata are introduced. Kata form the backbone of the traditional martial arts instructional approach (Friday, 1995). Popularly understood as "forms," kata are a series of movements combined into a performance set. Most traditional martial arts organizations, whether bujutsu or budo systems, have a corpus of individual kata that are learned by trainees at various points in their study. Mastery of individual kata is often linked to promotion. Thus, kata are ways to develop student skill.

Kata are more than just performance routines designed to polish technique or showcase ability, however. They are also thought to embody lessons learned by past masters. When we consider that, in feudal Japan, a warrior's skill was often proven on the battlefield with lethal finality, the role of kata as non-lethal re-enactments of battlefield experience becomes much more understandable. So, too, can we appreciate the reason why kata training was held in such high regard by traditional proponents of the bujutsu.

But there is also merit to other attempts at technical application. Thus it is that many martial arts systems insist on a combat simulation that serves as a test of skill, variously labeled *taryu jidai*, *jiyu-renshu*, *shiai*, or *randori*. Whether between fighters from rival schools (as in the first term) or students of the same art, these free-fighting bouts are also designed to test the degree to which a trainee has mastered the martial arts curriculum. Especially in the modern age, when the brutally decisive evaluation of the battlefield was no longer a regular feature of training, budo systems attempted to replicate the challenge of real combat. Given their nature as relatively structured, quasi-sport systems, these bouts were highly conditioned, but none the less vigorous for all that. Especially in some of the more sport-oriented systems, such as judo and kendo, competitive sparring is a central feature of training, and a required part of grading qualifications.

So the martial arts curriculum is one composed of underlying principles (timing, distance breathing, body management) combined with specific techniques. Students are required to acquire proficiency in these actions along a well prescribed path, and to demonstrate mastery at increasing levels of sophistication, typically embodied in the kata series of a particular martial art style. Performance is judged in the context of isolated basics, a series of increasingly complex formal exercises, and more fluid, free-form self-defense or sparring situations.

EDUCATIONAL COMPONENTS

I have outlined the basic content of the martial curriculum. But as the label *bugei* or "martial art" suggests, training in these systems (whether bujutsu or budo) is as much about process as about result. There is an esthetic to both the action and product. We turn now to an exploration of the dynamics of the educational process in the dojo.

A Voluntary Process with Mixed Motivations

In the first place, study is voluntary. While school children in Japan are still required to take judo or kendo in school, further training is a result of individual initiative. This is certainly the case in the West, where martial arts training halls fall within the category of "voluntary organizations." Participation presupposes willingness to study, often because of some perceived benefit. The motivations for training are as varied as the trainees themselves, but we may isolate some common themes.

Some students approach the martial arts as exotic forms of exercise. In this regard, study forms part of a larger approach to healthy living. Those of us who have trained in these arts for any length of time, after inventorying the bruises, broken bones, etc. involved may wonder whether there are other activities that create less wear and tear, but it remains that martial arts training is considered by many as a calisthenic activity.

A stereotypical idea about martial arts trainees is that they are (or were originally) weak, timid people seeking some measure of confidence in self-defense situations. In the West, the allure of fighting skills often forms a part in martial arts marketing. We might note in passing that this idea is not seriously entertained in Japan. As has been suggested elsewhere (Donohue and Taylor, 1994), martial arts systems, whether bujutsu or budo, armed or unarmed, are anachronistic combat systems ill-suited for the reality of the modern battlefield or of contemporary society. Interested parties looking for some insight into how professional soldiers view budo are directed to read Heckler's 1990 account of trying to get Green Berets to practice aikido. The Japanese, who witnessed the historical spectacle of a band of die-hard swordsmen being cut to pieces by a peasant conscript army wielding firearms during the Satsuma Rebellion in 1876, retain no real illusions about the utility of the martial arts in normal circumstances. But for Westerners, the hint of Asian mystery and the promise of arcane mastery embodied in every cheap grade B martial arts movie keeps this questionable self-defense motivation alive.

As some budo forms adopted more sportive elements, the attraction of competition is also present as a motivator. Judo and kendo are budo systems that have the most well-developed contest emphasis, although karate continues to evolve in this area as well. Certainly the recent introduction of taekwondo (despite its Korean affiliation, it has been heavily influenced by Japanese empty-hand systems) in the Olympic games suggests that this trend is accelerating. While purists may bemoan an overemphasis on tournament participation as opposed to the more lofty pursuit of personal refinement, it must be acknowledged that the challenges and (largely intrinsic) rewards of competition serve to attract some students and keep them motivated through the relatively long period of training in the martial arts.

Not all bugei forms have opted for competitive practices, however. Traditional bujutsu systems consider them exercises in delusion. Within budo, arts like aikido and iaido are, in general, far more focused on these systems as mechanisms for personal development. There is considerable variation in competitive emphasis among other budo forms as well, and many schools have found that a greater stress on the "do" aspect of budo widens the appeal of the art for students without the competitive drive, requisite athletic ability, or sheer physical capacity for the tournament scene. In addition, popular ideas regarding physical activity, lifestyle, etc. seem to have attracted large numbers of students who would not normally participate in other, less exotic sport activities. In clinical terms, many non-competitive martial artists seem to be seeking the type of "flow experience" documented by Csikszentmihalyi (1975, 1990).

In short, there appear to be as many different reasons for studying martial arts as there are martial artists. The very flexibility of their emphases permits these systems to accommodate a wide variety of individual motivations. Yet, despite the personal motivation to participate, we also note an extremely high drop-out rate. Personal experience, as well as informal polling of other martial artists, suggests that probably only 10-20% of beginning students persist even to the very basic achievement of the first dan level. A 90% attrition rate was reported by Mas Oyama, founder of Kyokushinkai karatedo (1973). These levels do not appear implausible—Hurst reports that, in one historical period, of 1,384 pupils who entered the Yabuchi-ryu of the tea ceremony, only 11 reached the level of *kaiden*, equivalent to an advanced dan ranking in modern budo (Hurst, 1995: 22).

A variety of factors contribute to this drop-out rate. Large proportions of beginning martial arts students are adolescents. The competing social, educational, and career demands that emerge over the years often pull trainees away. Financial considerations (participation comes at a price) may also interfere. More significant than that, however, may be contrast created between the reality of martial arts training and the stereotypical expectations many people bring with them.

Movie industry glamour aside, most martial arts training is decidedly difficult. In addition, the process of achieving technical competence is rather lengthy, even for gifted athletes. The rewards of practice are largely personal ones that yield little or no material or social benefit for the martial artist. In short, the process of learning the martial arts, despite the overly romanticized fantasies of adolescents, appears to offer little to individuals raised in a consumer culture. Where public tastes dictate speed and ease, the arts are hard to master and advancement is slow. In a society where achievement is meant to be conspicuously paraded (and hopefully converted into wealth), martial artists look no different from anyone else and typically never exhibit their skills outside the bounds of a training hall.

Despite the seemingly contrarian nature of the martial arts in terms of the popular trends of modern society, we note a relatively constant interest in these phenomena for the last 25 years. Motivations include all the factors discussed above, and have been fueled at least in part by mass communications. I would also suggest that the fact that the martial arts appear to run counter to the prevailing values of society can account for their fascination particularly among young people, who form the majority of practitioners. In addition, I have noted (Donohue, 1994) that Western cultural emphases on the importance of individualism, the cultural and historical linkages established between violence and freedom (whether you are discussing *Butch Cassidy and the Sundance Kid* or *Robin of Locksley*), a search for mystic enlightenment, as well as a human psychological predisposition to seek "flow" experiences, can help account for the popularity of the martial arts.

Rolling Admissions

An important feature of martial arts training is that it is possible to begin training at any time. While some traditional bujutsu schools in Japan require formal introductions, recommendations, etc. to be accepted as a student, most contemporary schools in the West require little other than interest, funds, and the ability to abide by the rules of the dojo.

There is thus no artificial structure, no seasonal orientation or ritual calendar that conditions the timing of a student's entrance. This openness reinforces the voluntary nature of the enterprise. We may also suspect that it is conditioned by the frequent phenomenon of discontinuous study by students due to school and career commitments. Finally, any organization with a 90% attrition rate had better accept students at any time.

Cyclical Curricula Based on Refinement of Basics

The fact that schools have a type of rolling admissions is made possible by the cyclical nature of the martial arts curriculum. There is, of course, some differentiation between beginning and advanced students in practice in terms of their activities. This is especially true in early stages of the arts when novices need to develop basic skills (such as falling safely, to use an example from judo). But the central distinction between beginners and more advanced students in terms of activity is one of degree, not kind. Thus, it is possible for trainees with a broad spectrum of skills to practice together.

The martial arts emphasis on fundamentals is responsible for this state of affairs. This is a pervasive educational pattern in traditional Japan. Friday (1995) suggests that the Confucian infatuation with ritual formalism is at least partly the cause. We might also note that the ideographic Chinese writing system demanded a mastery of literally thousands of characters, and a type of fundamental precision was needed to engage in any literary activity. Given the dominant place of Confucianism in Tokugawa Japan, it is not surprising that the rigor of this approach to instruction informed other areas as well.

The modern martial arts, whose fundamental characteristics were shaped by Tokugawa paradigms, are no exception. All trainees, at whatever level, are expected to continue to practice the building blocks of their particular art for a lifetime. These basic elements form the vocabulary of the martial conversation and, as such, need to be continuously polished. Many the newly minted karate black belt is surprised, on being awarded dan rank, to being re-introduced to the same kata begun as a white belt.

In the martial arts there is an explicit belief that the amazing prowess of the master is one that has been forged slowly, over time. It is not a mysterious event. Although it is a suprarational process, it is the anticipated outcome of practice, refinement, and ruthless self-criticism. The traditional martial arts of Japan reject the "quick and easy" formulations of mass-marketing and run counter to the ostensibly progressive admonitions of Bruce Lee to "absorb what is useful" (1975). The techniques and kata of the art are accepted by trainees as embodying critical martial lessons. The fact that many of these lessons take years to fully grasp does nothing to devalue them. In Japanese martial arts training, it is an article of faith that mastery of basics creates advanced competence. Only when trainees have mastered *ji*, the outward manifestation of the internal lessons of an art, are they free to abandon the style's strictures and display pure *ri*, the underlying principle.

Finally, the pace of this process of mastery is determined by the aptitude of the pupil. The absence of a temporal structure to the training cycle, combined with the nature of the curriculum itself, means that students are (within limits) free to acquire mastery at their own speed. Differing physical capacities, emotional maturity and psychological factors create varying dynamics for each student. Any experienced martial arts instructor knows that there are fairly consistent patterns in aggregate learning, but that each student brings a unique set of strengths and weaknesses to the process. The cyclical nature of training permits general progression to take place while at the same time permitting individual focus on specific deficiencies.

An Applications Orientation

Martial arts are relentlessly performance oriented. While their theory is complex and the ideology often fascinating, it is in the doing that these arts are revealed. A martial artist who talks too much about the art is generally suspect. In the dojo, it is not philosophy, but function, that is foremost.

This stress is reinforced through all the art's components. The mastery of basics is expressed through their combination in kata and their application in the more fluid situations of free sparring and contest. Considerable disagreement persists among martial artists regarding the "reality" of sport contest as opposed to real combat. No modern martial artist seriously contends, for instance, that a kendo *shiai* is exactly like *shinken shobu*, a fight with real swords. Nonetheless, the modern introduction of competitive fighting in budo can be understood as a partial attempt to retain the vigor and mental focus of combat for contemporary trainees.

Direction by a Master Teacher

Unlike the stereotypical portrait of a teacher established by Mark Twain, in the world of the martial arts, the sensei is able to both teach and do. While the respect for an instructor is certainly partially conditioned by traditional Japanese notions of appropriate behavior due one's social superiors, in the dojo it also colored by the fact that the sensei embodies the skills and behavior the trainee seeks. In this sense, the sensei is not merely a coach or trainer, but a model.

The psychological and physical dominance of the sensei over trainees forms a notable feature of martial arts instruction and shares much in common with the complex psycho-physical dominance of a military drill instructor over recruits. It is built on trust that the instructor, who has mastered the art in question, is capable of leading the novice down that same difficult path. The instructor poses challenges and provides clues as to their solution. Guidance is accepted by the student because, as a model of achievement, the instructor's insights are validated and simultaneously create hope that the goal of mastery is attainable for the novice as well.

Standards-Oriented

Due to the functional orientation of the martial arts, technical standards are well-defined and objective within systems. A caveat is necessary here. I do not mean to imply universal agreement across styles—one merely has to look at the variety of front stances used in karate styles to put this notion to rest—nor to ignore the fact that the commercialization of the martial arts has led to some deterioration of standards. Within individual schools in the Japanese tradition, however, consistent systemic approaches to evaluating skill are the norm.

The skills and behaviors required for promotion are clearly modeled in the training hall. The sensei and the senior students all provide novices with examples of technical competency. Conformity to the model and a fidelity to its principles are relentlessly insisted on. Personal interpretation or stylistic elaboration by students is frowned upon—not surprising in a culture that maintains that "the nail that sticks out gets banged down."

Finally, competence is never assumed. Due to the physical nature of the arts, ability has to be demonstrated. Such demonstrations are often public in nature. In an additional attempt to preserve stylistic uniformity and maintain standards, some arts require tests for advanced ranks to be taken at public gatherings of many schools, with an examining board of senior instructors. This ensures greater objectivity in evaluating students and reinforces common standards through an act of public group conformity.

Transcendent Intent

Finally, the entire activity of martial arts training is thought of as having a type of transcendent intent. The demands these arts place on trainees in terms of time and effort, as well as the fact that they are not, in the context of the modern world, practical or efficient military arts, require an overarching purpose that transcends the mere physical. Certainly a portion of the attraction these systems hold is their ideology. While subject to various interpretations, most martial arts extant share certain broad convictions. Especially for modern budo, there is an explicit suggestion that training contains within it the potential for a type of transcendence (Van Horne, 1996).

A basic (and Confucian) idea is that striving to master complex tasks can help improve character. The "superior man" of Confucian ideology had mastered a number of skills, and this search for refinement was expected to have a direct impact on the individual. With the decline in strict military utility, the martial arts came to be viewed by the Japanese as training vehicles to strengthen and improve the human character. Part of this attitude was the residual effect of an association of military arts with the upper class in Japan, but the modern era also ushered in a period of dramatic change that made the Japanese nostalgic for traditional practices. Although synthesized contemporary versions of martial systems, budo preserved conservative patterns of dress, deportment, and action that made them mechanisms for cultural preservation.

Thoughtful samurai had been reflecting with some sophistication on the deeper implications of their calling since at least the sixteenth century. Indigenous Japanese ideas in Shinto regarding pervasive forces and universal principles, as well as Daoist and esoteric Buddhist influences assisted in the development of mystical practices associated with martial training that span the spectrum from chanting, spells, meditation, and secret hand gestures, to attempts to cultivate the life force known as *ki*. The influence of Zen, while relatively recent, is the logical (and vague) extension of this trend. By virtue of its focus on direct experience, Zen suggests a form of enlightenment that can be attained by sudden realization or through long training. Although technically a form of Buddhism, Zen's (theoretical) rejection of specific scripture has made it a perfectly non-threatening ideological component to the martial arts as they have spread beyond Japan. The emphasis on these ideological factors varies from art to art, but all generally acknowledge some validity in each aspect.

ALL THE MYRIAD WAYS: EDUCATIONAL PARALLELS

When a modern educator looks at the martial arts, he is presented with a type of instructional model. Some aspects of this model have been created by the vagaries of historical happenstance, but their persistence, and especially their perpetuation in non-Japanese cultural environments around the world, suggest some functionality. As a college instructor who grapples with the elusive waza of the mind with my students in college classrooms and who also teaches martial arts, I am constantly comparing teaching and learning in the classroom and in the dojo. I am also increasingly convinced that there is method in the madness of the martial arts.

This point was brought home to me when I was asked recently to develop an analysis of and rationale for organizational hierarchy in martial arts instruction (Donohue, 1998b). Drafting my argument for an audience that was decidedly non-traditional in orientation, as well as for an editor who thought there was no difference between teaching scuba diving and the martial arts and who also saw little or no value in the "old" ways, through our debate I developed an enhanced appreciation for the sophistication of martial arts pedagogy.

Let us examine the salient features I have outlined and see how they connect with contemporary discussions on teaching and learning in higher education.

Voluntary Participation

While some level of formal education is mandatory in the countries of the industrialized world, higher education is an option, not a requirement, for people. In this sense, it partakes of the voluntary situation encountered in martial arts dojo.

Despite this voluntary aspect, the level and type of motivation present in individual students is varied. Just as there are many differing motivations for studying the martial arts, so, too, are reasons for attending college different from person to person. We might venture to say that the mixture of motives is a reflection of the expectation that a high proportion of young people will attend college or university. Certainly in the United States, education beyond the high school level is the anticipated norm, not the exception.

Parallels also exist in that many college students, like novice martial artists, don't clearly understand the true purpose of training or have different issues in mind. They bring to their work a host of assumptions and expectations, some accurate, some fanciful, some that prove impediments to advancement. This is one of the reasons why attrition remains a significant problem in both endeavors. How fall-out is perceived differs in the two organizations, however.

While higher education administrators constantly view the issue of attrition as a problem to be solved, martial arts sensei understand that this phenomenon is part of the process of learning. In my own position I am constantly called upon to ameliorate student drop-out rates. Counseling, tutoring, and various proactive gymnastics are brought to bear. We even have a course that "teaches" students how to be students.

The sensei, on the other hand, watches impassively as students lose or find their way. Given the variety of possible motivators for study, the process of training acts to clarify the true nature of the endeavor for the beginner and clearly establishes the elements and actions that will be needed for success. Attrition or persistence is the result as disillusionment or insight takes place for the individual. In higher education, on the other hand, attrition is viewed as the abrupt and improper end of learning. In the dojo, it is the result of the learning process itself.

Despite the difficulties both areas of endeavor pose for students, they continue to attract people. Indeed, there are some fundamental commonalities between the rigor of the liberal arts and the martial arts (Levine, 1984). Both categories are systemic and organized, and offer the individual a mechanism for exerting some control over the world. They require discipline, effort, and fidelity of purpose. Above all, they possess both utilitarian and transcendent purpose. Psychologists have established that a type of endeavor that engages both mind and body in complex activity that is challenging and yet not impossible, holds tremendous intrinsic attraction for individuals (Csikszentmihalyi, 1975). Higher education and martial arts training can be categorized as things that have the potential for being what are termed "flow" activities.

A Cyclical Training Pattern

Traditional higher education differs significantly from martial arts training in this regard. Temporal divisions and discrete training periods are the norm. Traditionally, the delivery of formal education has been linked to, and organized around, the agricultural cycle. Education is doled out in segments according to a fixed, yet abstract, schedule. It is used in lower grades to assure that material presented and tasks required are appropriate for the cognitive development of students at different ages. At this level it is appropriate, since it is related directly to biological and psychological factors.

Higher education preserves this formal temporal organization, chopping up learning into courses, semesters, quarters, terms, years etc., but the appropriate developmental rationale present in elementary and secondary education is missing. At college and university, this arrangement is maintained mostly for ease of processing. The suggestion that higher education is both an educational endeavor and business enterprise should come as no surprise to us. Institutional mottos to the contrary, most colleges and universities are oriented around bureaucratic issues—regularity, manageability, efficiency—not educational excellence. The approach in many institutions of higher learning that I am familiar with is to set students a task to be achieved in an abstract space of time. Faster learning is not rewarded. Slower learning is punished. For many students, the experience is analogous to working on the assembly line floor—a numbing series of disconnected tasks achieved with mediocre efficiency, but little emotional investment. If some students seem to have lost sight of the purpose and joy of learning, it is probably because institutions have set up conditions that would seem to suggest that their professors have forgotten as well.

We are today witnessing some modification of this approach. In the U.S., more than half of all college students are "non-traditional" in terms of their age or the ways in which they "consume" a college education. Institutions have increasingly begun to experiment with alternative delivery systems. Internet technology, in particular, has accelerated this process, introducing the possibility of the asynchronic classroom and virtual universities. The University of Phoenix, a for-profit educational institution that delivers coursework on-line, is today the largest private university in the United States. While we may well reserve judgement as to the ultimate appropriateness of using computers to mold minds, we see here an attempt to introduce more flexibility into the organization of instructional systems.

An Applications Orientation

As part of a movement against the factory-like organization of learning, educational trends in higher education are increasingly focused on "outcomes." In this, it would seem as if education is adopting some of the emphasis found in the dojo.

But, in the U.S., this development has been spawned by largely negative factors. One is the fact that undergraduates are taking longer to complete their degree programs, so the time-limited orientation is no longer as useful as it was in years past. In addition, research regarding psychological factors in learning, as well as legal mandates in the area of disabilities, have created a greater sensitivity to individual learning differences. Hence the advent of discussions of "learning styles" and "multiple intelligences" (Gardner, 1983, 1993; Armstrong, 1994) and an emphasis on using different means to attain the same educational results.

In addition, in the United States, public perception of the failure of educational organizations to produce minimally competent graduates—corporate America spends $5 billion in retraining new employees in the mysteries of basic mathematics and expository writing—has created a movement that stresses the finite measurement of "competencies" in the academic setting. In an emphasis on outcomes assessment, the "relevance" of courses of study to careers, and a variety of innovations that attempt to link the abstract world of the school to the concrete world of labor, educational institutions begin to resemble martial arts systems in terms of their focus on performance.

Yet, interestingly enough, the pedagogical sophistication of educational institutions seems somewhat limited when compared to martial arts systems. Unlike the bugei, where an appreciation of outcomes is nicely balanced with an emphasis on the process of learning, educators often seem caught in a binary mind set, where only one of two options can be stressed. This has led, in some cases, to an over-emphasis on the product and a total neglect of the fundamental elements of competence that are embedded in the process of learning.

To a certain extent, we can understand this is a logical extension of a consumer mentality. Whether in the martial arts dojo or the school, people focus on the end result: the black belt's skills, the graduate's competencies. These things, after all, assist in creating a motivation for study. In a world that increasingly values ease, speed, and immediate gratification, approaches to learning that focus on the final outcome often de-emphasize and neglect the labor that typically leads to mastery.

In the martial arts, the traditional sequence of learning is expressed as *shu-ha-ri*, concepts which suggest that students must first master the basics of the art before they are able to grasp the underlying principles of mastery. Various commentators on martial systems (Otaki and Draeger, 1983; Friday, 1995; Monday, 1994; Hurst, 1995) agree on the fundamental nature of this concept in training. In addition, a dominant element in the training paradigm is the expectation that the individual trainee must conform to the learning process and technical approach as established by the group (Van Horne, 1996). In other words, the short-term expectations of the individual for quick and easy mastery are overcome by the corporate insistence on a long-term developmental process that stresses competence in basics as a path to mastery.

Educators in the non-martial realm seem to have difficulty with this balance, feeling that popular demands for easy competence suggest that the difficult and tedious work of basic learning can somehow be done away with. The case of an approach to reading known as Whole Language, in which elementary students are expected to learn to read English by visual cues, context, and suggestions from illustrations as opposed to phonics-based methods, is a case in point. By abandoning the phonetic fundamentals of reading skills, educators have created a false expectation of easy mastery. In the process, they have created a disastrous decline in reading ability in school districts where Whole Language has been adopted.

Commentators on higher education note a similar attempt at short-circuiting basic work, plunging students into complex interdisciplinary endeavors while neglecting to provide them with the basic knowledge and skill sets necessary to grapple with sophisticated subjects. Critics of American higher education like Bloom (1987) cite the absence of concrete standards and common knowledge sets as resulting in a virtual intellectual shutdown, while Barzun (1991) suggests that, in our failure to balance educational product with educational process, we have forgotten how to both teach and learn.

In this regard, it would seem as if education has something to learn from the world of the martial arts. It should come as no surprise to learn that these systems, focused as they are on issues of physical movement and human potential, should exhibit a sensitivity to the concept of balance in the form and substance of the training endeavor.

Instruction by a Master Teacher

The absolutely vital role of the martial arts sensei in the training of students is a universal feature of these systems. As I have indicated, the special educational dynamic that is created here is a result of both psychological and physiological factors. The sensei is a living model for trainees, an absolute judge of competence, and the embodiment of hope that the seemingly impossible skill required is, in fact, attainable.

In Education, the recognition that "master teachers" can play a vital role in pedagogy is offset by a real shortage of individuals who fit the bill. At the elementary and secondary levels, prospective teachers score uniformly low in aptitude tests and standardized measurements of academic ability—and have done so since the 1920's (Sowell, 1993: 25). At the university level, it is often the case that undergraduate instruction is left to graduate students while accomplished scholars conduct research and pursue writing interests. At smaller colleges with a more pronounced "career" focus, the process of professionalization and credentialing needed for a professorial career often isolates instructors from the fields they are training people in.

The result in the classroom is a dearth of role models for learners. Unlike the martial arts dojo, where the sensei occupies a status position continually validated by performance, classroom instruction typically exhibits an absence of modeled behavior. This leads to a decline in respect for instructors and their subjects, and fosters an attitude that the effort needed to master these topics or develop these skills is not worth it, since the activity is judged not relevant to "real" needs.

In short, dojo instruction tends to work in part because the instructor embodies the outcome students seek, models the behavior and skills of the art in question, and serves as a guide in the developmental process. This dynamic is one that could be much more successfully adopted in the classroom.

Standards-Oriented

Part of the central mechanism for martial arts training is a continuous stress on basic skills, their refinement and utilization in the process of mastery. Education in the classroom is also focused on process, but in the sense of "processing" student through a series of credentialed steps that take place according to a specific timetable. Like an object on an assembly line, a student is propelled through a series of experiences and required to demonstrate isolated "competencies." A central feature of contemporary education for many students is a lack of a sense of connectedness or integration of the various "outcomes."

This creates some rather high frustration levels for learners in the classroom. As a result, teachers have embraced a "learning styles" orientation that reduces structure for students, and focuses on the outcome of the learning process. Ironically, since all learners are assumed to bring different strengths to the process—the seven multiple intelligences of Gardner's (1983) theory—there is little uniformity in the way these outcomes are expressed. This paves the way for a deterioration of standards, cloaked as sensitivity.

While one could argue that this is a type of instructional strategy, it is hardly efficient, humane, or likely to lead to skill mastery. The very vagueness of the modern educational enterprise ensures that the shortcomings of such an approach will take some time to reveal themselves. Not so in the world of the martial arts. Imagine, if you will, a judo instructor omitting a novice's instruction in *ukemi* (falling) and merely expecting the student to learn at his own pace or in his own way how to fall properly. Over a period of time, through observation and participation in the school of "hard knocks" some pupils would learn. But at what cost in injury, wasted time, and diminished technical competence? If the judo instructor were to accept the idea that some students lacked a type of "ukemi intelligence" and should not be required to exhibit this skill, he would, in fact, be engaging in a type of instructional malpractice. In fact, one of Kano's central innovations in developing judo was a detailed educational program that taught students how to fall safely. While many jujutsu schools of the time did not do this, Kano felt such an approach was inefficient. He was right, and consequently developed a systematic instructional approach that forces students to conform to a method of learning and demonstrating specific basic skills.

Nonetheless, many modern educators, fixated on end competencies and unwilling to subject students to the hard work of mastering basic skills, continue to advocate the type of approach Kano rejected over a century ago. This is the case with pedagogical fads such as Whole Language and the pervasive desire to make all educational activity "relevant"—which in educational usage of the day carries with it the sense of effortless fun. While one could argue that any learning experience is relevant, contemporary educators often make the error of letting students judge the importance and relevance of things. This results in the untrained directing the curriculum.

Even in higher education, increasing numbers of courses are "interdisciplinary" in nature or require no prerequisite knowledge base. As a result, an emphasis on mastery of basic knowledge sets and intellectual skills is increasingly absent. Critics like Hirsch (1988) and Bloom (1987) would advocate the perspective that this problem has reached epidemic proportions. While they suggest that the appalling deterioration of standards in the American classroom is tinged by a political agenda, we can leave this contentious argument aside and merely note that the structure of education and the dictates of consumer culture—make life easy, strive for immediate gratification, and serve the uninformed (or artificially created) needs of the customer—would seem to make this development inevitable.

Martial artists, too, are big believers in relevance. In the martial arts dojo, however, there is no such tyranny by the trainee. The sensei directs the process of skill acquisition. By virtue of his status as a master teacher, his pupils trust his judgement, even though they may not always immediately grasp the direct applicability of what they are practicing. The confidence of martial arts teachers in providing students with a well-defined process for learning, and the acceptance by trainees of the considerable strictures this process entails, is considerably different from the case in many classrooms today.

Transcendent Mission

To my mind, the greatest contrast between martial pedagogy and traditional education has to do with the question of transcendent mission. In many ways, martial artists are seeking something from their training that goes beyond mere technique, and they are implicitly convinced that these arts can, in some way, lead them to what they seek. In addition, the sensei, exuding confidence in the system and serving as a living embodiment of skill and accomplishment, seems to validate the reality of the trainee's hope.

In such an environment, an insistence on conformity to specific etiquette and techniques is not perceived as arbitrary or worthless. The fact that specific skills are difficult to master does not detract from their worth, but rather enhances them. An instructor's insistence that a pupil be able to consistently demonstrate specific skills is not sadistic rigidity or oppression. They are all, rather, important steps on the way to mastery.

Contrast this to contemporary classrooms. Students passively endure their years in school. They are often there because they have to be or, in the case of higher education, because they understand education as a means to an economic end. Often overlooked are the humanistic dimensions of education, the expansion of intellectual horizons and the shared joy in learning the lessons of the human experience. Increasingly, as the critic Neal Postman comments, schools are places of detention, not attention (1996).

In addition, as educational organizations have become more intent on accommodating a variety of learning styles, they have also become much more flexible in terms of educational ideology. In a familiar post-modern dilemma, academics, in face of the alternatives, seem powerless to choose. The result is an educational environment with very few clearly stated and commonly shared goals. The growing lack of structure in education (and it is no accident that "deconstructionism" was a recent intellectual fad in higher education), creates a crisis of faith, not only in the central mission of education, but even in the belief that we are capable of identifying such a thing at all. This state of affairs is as much a causal factor as it is a symptom of our problems.

Despite what many people understand as a crass concern with combat, the various Japanese martial systems have all developed philosophical rationales that elevate these activities from the realm of simple instrumentality. As a result, students come to perceive a transcendent purpose in training that makes the challenge of the process eminently valuable: it is leading not only to specific skills, but also to something larger than the self. In the process, it provides individuals with an enhanced sense of identity and purpose.

The irony of martial arts training, of course, is that such a complex and effective pedagogical technique is embedded in activities that are typically thought of as either wholly devoted to the celebration of force or as esoteric encounters with the Mystic East. In fact, the martial arts are complex forms of human endeavor that preserve and perpetuate insight, join people together in common purpose and, through carefully structured training, enmesh individuals in activities that celebrate the potential of the human mind and spirit.

In short, what one can experience in the dojo is the sort of transformative event that the most romantic of us hoped to encounter in the university. The only difference is that, in the dojo, the process has a much greater likelihood of helping you reach your goal.

BIBLIOGRAPHY

Armstrong, T. (1994). *Multiple intelligences in the classroom*. Alexandria, VA: Association for Supervision and Curriculum Development.

Barzun, J. (1991). *Begin here: The forgotten conditions of teaching and learning*. Chicago: University of Chicago Press.

Bloom, H. (1987). *The closing of the American mind*. New York: Simon and Schuster.

Csikszentmihalyi, M. (1990). *Flow: The psychology of optimal experience*. New York: Harper and Row.

Csikszentmihalyi , M. (1975). *Beyond boredom and anxiety: The experience of play and work in games*. San Francisco: Josey-Bass.

Donohue, J. (1999). *Complete kendo*. Boston: Charles E. Tuttle.

Donohue, J. (1998a). *Herding the ox: The martial arts as moral metaphor*. Wethersfield, CT: Turtle Press.

Donohue, J. (1998b). What is healthy martial arts hierarchy. In Corcoran, J. and J. Graden (eds.) *ACMA Instructor Certification Manual*. St. Petersburg,

FL: Graden Media Communications Group, pp. 127-136.

Donohue, J. (1997). Ideological elasticity: Enduring form and changing function in the Japanese martial tradition. *Journal of Asian Martial Arts* 6(2): 10-25.

Donohue, J. (1994) *Warrior dreams: The martial arts and the American imagination*. Westwood, CT: Bergin and Garvey.

Donohue, J. (1991a). *The forge of the spirit: Structure, motion, and meaning in the Japanese martial tradition*. New York: Garland Publishing.

Donohue, J. (1991b). The dimensions of discipleship: Organizational paradigm, mystical transmission, and vested interest in the Japanese martial tradition. *Ethnos*, 55: 1-2.

Donohue, J. (1990). Training halls of the Japanese martial tradition: A symbolic analysis of budo dojo in New York. *Anthropos*, 85: 55-63.

Donohue, J. (1988). Sword magic: Belief, form, and function in the Japanese martial tradition. *Human Affairs*, 14: 9-35.

Donohue, J. and Taylor, K. (1994). The classification of the fighting arts. *Journal of Asian Martial Arts*, 3(4): 10-37.

Dore, R. (1965). *Education in Tokugawa Japan*. Berkeley: University of California Press.

Draeger, D. (1974). *Modern bujutsu and budo*. New York: John Weatherhill.

Draeger, D. (1973a). *Classical budo*. New York: John Weatherhill.

Draeger, D. (1973b). *Classical bujutsu*. New York: John Weatherhill.

Draeger, D., and Smith, R. (1989). *Comprehensive Asian fighting arts*. New York: Kodansha.

Friday, K. (1997). *Legacies of the sword: The Kashima Shinryu and martial culture*. Honolulu: University of Hawai'i Press.

Friday, K. (1995). Kabala in motion: Kata and pattern practice in the traditional bugei. *Journal of Asian Martial Arts*, 4(4): 26-39.

Funakoshi, G. (1973). *Karate-do kyohan: The master text*. Tokyo: Kodansha.

Fussell, P. (1992). *Bad or, the dumbing of America*. NY: Touchstone Books.

Gardner, H. (1993). *Multiple intelligences: The theory in practice*. New York: Basic Books.

Gardner, H. (1983). *Frames of mind: The theory of multiple intelligences*. New York: Basic Books.

Heckler, R. (1990). *In search of the warrior spirit*. Berkeley, CA: North Atlantic.

Hirsch, E. (1988). *Cultural literacy*. New York: Vintage Books.

Hsu, F. (1975). *Iemoto: The heart of Japan*. Cambridge: Belknap Press.

Hurst, G. (1998). *Armed martial arts of Japan*. New Haven, CT: Yale University Press.

Hurst, G. (1995). Ryuha in the martial and other Japanese arts. *Journal of*

Asian Martial Arts, 4(4): 12-25.

Hurst, G. (1990). From heiho to bugei: Emergence of the martial arts in Tokugawa Japan. Paper presented at the 6th Annual Conference, Society for the Anthropological Study of Consciousness, Pacific Palisades, CA.

Kano, J., et. al. (1986). *Kodokan Judo*. Tokyo: Kodansha.

King, W. (1993). *Zen and the way of the sword: Arming the Samurai psyche*. Oxford: Oxford University Press.

Lee, B. (1975). *The Tao of Jeet Kun Do*. Burbank: Ohara Publishing.

Leggett, T. (1978). *Zen and the ways*. Rutland, VT: Charles E. Tuttle.

Levine, D. (1984). The liberal arts and the martial arts. *Liberal Education*, 70(3): 235-251.

Maliszewski, M. (1998). *Spiritual dimensions of the martial arts*. Boston: Charles E. Tuttle.

Monday, N. (1994). The ryu ha system: Continuity and change in Japanese martial culture. *Journal of Asian Martial Arts*, 3(1): 72-81.

O'Neill, P. (1984). Organization and authority in the traditional arts. *Modern Asian Studies*, 18(4): 631-645.

Otaki, T., and Draeger, D. (1983). *Judo formal techniques: A complete guide to Kodokan randori no kata*. Rutland: Charles E. Tuttle.

Nakane, C. (1970). *Japanese society*. Berkeley: University of California Press.

Oyama, M. (1973). *This is karate*. Tokyo: Japan Publishing.

Pieter, W. (1994). Research in martial sports: A review. *Journal of Asian Martial Arts*, 3(2): 10-47.

Pieter, W. (1993). Body and mind in medieval and pre-modern Japanese martial arts. *Journal of Asian Martial Arts*, 2(4): 10-27.

Postman, N. (1996). *The end of education*. New York: Alfred A. Knopf.

Ratti, O., and Westbrook, A. (1973). *Secrets of the samurai*. Rutland, VT: Charles E. Tuttle.

Sasamori, J., and Warner, G. (1964). *This is kendo*. Rutland, VT: Charles E. Tuttle.

Sowell, T. (1993). *Inside American education*. New York: Free Press.

Stevens, J. (1984). *Abundant peace: The life of Morihei Ueshiba, founder of Aikido*. Boulder, CO: Shambhala.

Suzuki, D. (1959). *Zen and Japanese culture*. Princeton, NJ: Princeton University Press.

Ueshiba, K. (1985). *Aikido*. Tokyo: Hozansha Publishing.

Van Horne, W. (1996). Ideal teaching: Japanese culture and the training of the warrior. *Journal of Asian Martial Arts*, 5(4): 10-19.

Varley, P. (1995). Samurai in school: Ryuha in traditional Japanese martial arts. *Journal of Asian Martial Arts*, 4(4): 10-11.

chapter 9

KAHO: CULTURAL MEANING AND EDUCATIONAL METHOD IN KATA TRAINING

by John J. Donohue, Ph.D.

The trainee stands garbed in the robes of a by-gone era, gripping a weapon as deadly as it is archaic. The world tightens down to a small universe built of hard wood, polished steel, cotton cloth, body heat, sweat, and the tidal pulse of heartbeat and respiration. Here, the weapon is wielded in a sequence of moves set down by masters long gone, actions refined and repeated until the performer is lost in the hiss of effort and the focused pursuit of perfection. It is a curious thing, part technical exercise, part performance art, part meditative experience. It is kata.

Introduction

The world of the Asian martial arts is one that has gripped the imagination of Westerners for decades now. Its trappings strike the outside viewer as exotic, its motivations arcane. It is dense with symbolism and occluded meaning. It is rife with opportunity for misunderstanding and romanticization. It is, in short, a social phenomenon that cries out for anthropological analysis.

Students of many modern Japanese martial arts are fond of reminding us, as the Japanese term *budo* implies, that they are really "martial ways." The destination of these ways is varied: they can be understood as systems of physical exercise or spiritual development, as relatively efficient physiological (as opposed to technological) systems, as recreational and competitive sports, or as civilian self-defense methods. In fact, any intense scrutiny of these systems reveals a multifaceted nature in which aspects of all these things can be recognized. The deeper the understanding of budo, the greater their recognized complexity.

This sophistication relates not merely to the techniques and systems themselves, but to the way in which they have been taught within the Japanese martial tradition. This represents another avenue of scientific inquiry for researchers focusing on sociological interpretations of martial arts activity.

I will examine the structure and purpose of the practice patterns known in the Japanese martial tradition as *kata*. While some Westerners have questioned the necessity for kata training, it continues to form a part of most orthodox martial systems. And the social scientist wonders "why?" This chapter examines *kaho* (the use of kata as an instructional tool) from two perspectives: kata training as a cultural activity that has been shaped by the structural characteristics of Japanese culture, and kata training as a highly developed and effective educational mechanism for imparting technical skill in the martial arts.

Practitioners of Motobo-ryu Udun-di, an Okinawan
style as taught by Uehara Seikichi, work together
on one of the nine empty-hand kata in the system.
Photograph courtesy of Richard Florence.

Kata

Kata forms the backbone of the Japanese traditional martial arts instructional approach (Friday, 1995: 1997). Popularly understood as "forms," kata are a series of movements combined into a performance set. Most traditional Japanese martial arts organizations and systems have a corpus of individual kata that trainees learn at various points in their study. Mastery of individual kata is often linked to promotion. Thus, kata are most immediately thought of as ways to develop student skill.

Haruna Matsuo, a Muso Jikiden Eishin-ryu instructor,
performing a sword opening and closing technique.
Photographs courtesy of Kim Taylor.

Kata are more than just performance routines designed to polish technique or showcase ability, however. They are also thought to embody lessons learned by past masters. When we consider that in feudal Japan a warrior's skill was often proven on the battlefield with lethal finality, the role of kata as non-lethal re-enactments of battlefield experience becomes much more understandable. So, too, can we appreciate the reason proponents of the traditional combat-oriented systems (often identified as *bujutsu*, "martial methods") held kata training in such high regard.

The teaching of combat skill, however, does not necessarily mandate such a highly structured, ritualistic approach. Western wrestlers and boxers, for instance, are not schooled through such elaborate patterns. Westerners practicing more modern martial arts systems have abandoned or de-emphasized kata in favor of what they consider more "realistic" and "practical" exercises. For these people, kata practice is a cultural relic, easily jettisoned. It is a contemporary urge for "relevance" that is quite familiar to educators. Yet kata practice persists in many Japanese martial systems practiced today. This persistence argues for a type of functionality that needs to be examined.

Cultural Factors

One source of kaho's continued endurance in the martial arts world may spring from the formative cultural environment of the martial arts. The organization of any human activity reflects its cultural context, and the Japanese martial traditions are no exception. Although the mechanics of fighting are considerably conditioned by human physiology and kinesiology, as well as by the weapons technology being applied, stylistic approaches and organizational patterns are culturally conditioned.

Kata are authoritative things. They are passed on from high-ranking instructors to novices. The criteria used to judge the performance of these sets is one that emphasizes a fidelity to form and movement within the dictates the instructor has established. The student's ability to imitate his teacher in kata performance is considered a key to advancement in rank and status. Kaho's stress of hierarchy, authority, organizational belonging, and conformity all resonate strongly with Japanese cultural patterns.

Indeed, in sociological terms, we can understand Japanese martial arts as corporate entities with a strongly hierarchical organization and an explicit ideological charter. These structural factors condition the process of training to a great degree and so bear some further discussion.

In the first place, Japanese martial arts seem to share a predilection for formal organization that can be contrasted to the approach in other Asian countries. From the Tokugawa Period (1603-1868) onward, we note a marked tendency for martial arts training to be organized in corporate entities (Hurst, 1998). Schools came to have both a physical location, the *dojo* (literally "way place," the training hall) as well as a formal identity. Traditional bujutsu systems were often referred to as *ryu* (literally "streams," which gives some sense of the idea of corporate perpetuation). Usage in more modern martial arts systems known as *budo* is a bit more varied: some systems maintain the *ryu* label, others use the more modern designation of *kan* (hall) such as in Kodokan judo or Shotokan karatedo, or *kai* (association) as in Kyokushinkai karatedo.

Whatever their labels, these organizations are hierarchical entities, in which issues of rank (related to skill and seniority) condition behavior. At the pinnacle of the organization is the teacher (*sensei*), who is contrasted with his disciples (*montei*). In addition to this gross distinction, there are finer gradations present as well. Students are enmeshed in a dualistic series of relationships between superiors and subordinates that are modeled on the teacher/student split and that echo general structural principles in Japanese society (Nakane, 1970). Thus, a series of relativistic links between seniors (*sempai*) and juniors (*kyohai*) also shapes behavior in the dojo (Donohue, 1991).

The stratified nature of martial arts organizations is reinforced through their well-known ranking systems. Awareness of rank in these organizations is often buttressed by elaborate symbolic means such as methods of address and ritual bowing. In some systems, elements of training uniforms or their color are used to denote status. The most well-known item of clothing associated with rank is the colored-belt system adopted in many modern budo forms. In this system, trainees are classified according to *kyu* (class) and *dan* (grade). While permutations in hue and numbering are almost as varied as schools themselves, beginners in *kyu* levels usually wear white belts and, as they progress in rank, are awarded a series of different colored belts, culminating in the black belt, a sign that the trainee has reached dan level.

As they are organized today, budo organizations share a commonality with a widespread organizational type in Japan, the *iemoto* ("household origin," the main house in the traditional arts; Hsu, 1975). Although the Japanese do not formally identify most martial arts organizations as iemoto proper, the arts possess the highly structured hierarchical organization based on personal links between masters and disciples that are central characteristics of iemoto organizations.

As formal organizations, martial arts systems also have an explicit ideological charter—a "mission statement" in the corporate jargon of our times. These charters certainly relate to the philosophical orientation of many Japanese martial arts forms. Broadly speaking, many martial arts, and particularly modern budo systems, are inspired by a mix of Shinto, Confucian, and Buddhist ideas that link training with a type of personal/spiritual development. Much has been made, of course, of the alleged link between Zen and the martial arts (Suzuki, 1960; King, 1993; Leggett, 1978). While it is certainly possible that this connection was important for selected martial artists, it is neither universal nor historically accurate.

Kendo players utilize kata practice to maintain realistic techniques in a safe way. *Photograph courtesy of John Donohue.*

In fact, while not for a moment calling into question the sincerity of modern martial artists, an objective assessment of martial arts charters reveal them to be vaguely formulated statements that present these arts as ways to advance the technical practice of the art in question, to celebrate human potential, and to advance causes as diffuse and universally unobjectionable as good sportsmanship and world peace. Charters of this type are useful in that they provide an overarching philosophical rationale (however diffuse) for what would otherwise be merely highly stylized calisthenics. In addition, these charters can be understood as the direct consequence of two things: the need to "rehabilitate" the martial arts after the Second World War and a related attempt to homogenize elements of indigenous Japanese ideology so as to be more easily accepted as these arts spread to the West. It is interesting that this diffuse mysticism has had an unexpected appeal for Westerners seeking alternatives to traditional Western belief systems.

Traditional Asian approaches to learning may also have reinforced an emphasis on *kaho*. Friday (1995) suggests that the Confucian infatuation with ritual formalism is at least partly the cause. We might also note that the ideographic Chinese writing system demanded a mastery of literally thousands of characters, and a type of fundamental precision was needed to engage in any literary activity. Given the dominant place of Confucianism in Tokugawa Japan, it is not surprising that the rigor of this approach to instruction informed other endeavors as well.

The modern martial arts, the fundamental characteristics of which were shaped by Tokugawa paradigms, are no exception. All trainees, at whatever level, are expected to continue to practice the building blocks of their particular art for a lifetime. These basic elements form the vocabulary of the martial conversation and, as such, need to be continuously polished. These building blocks tend to be embedded in kata. Many a newly minted karate black belt is surprised, on being awarded dan rank, to being re-introduced to the same kata begun as a white belt. Kaho's stress on repetition, rote learning, and stylistic conformity fit very well within the Confucian tradition.

General cultural emphasis on age and seniority also shape *kaho*. Students tend to learn differing kata in a sequence that is tied to advancement in rank. Their models are "senior" students. And the higher the rank, the more complex the kata and the longer the period of time needed to master it. In the martial arts, there is an explicit belief that the amazing prowess of the master is one that has been forged slowly, over time. It is not a mysterious event. Although it is a suprarational process, it is the anticipated outcome of practice, refinement, and ruthless self-criticism. The traditional martial arts of Japan reject the "quick and easy" formulations of mass-marketing and run counter to the ostensibly progressive admonitions of Bruce Lee to "absorb what is useful" (1975). The techniques and kata of the art are accepted by trainees as embodying critical martial lessons. The fact that many of these lessons take years to fully grasp does nothing to devalue them. But it once again tends to reinforce a predilection for hierarchy, and *kaho* fits easily with such an expectation.

Rick Polland practicing Shindo Muso-ryu's standardized forms for the short staff (*jo*). *Photographs courtesy of R. Polland.*

Dr. Thomas Cauley, Director of the International Division of Sakugawa Koshiki Shorinji-ryu Karatedo, practicing a long staff (*bo*) kata. A few of his students practicing in unison. *Photographs courtesy of Wayne Van Horne.*

KAHO AS TECHNICAL SYSTEM

Certainly the traditional reliance on *kaho* as a centerpiece of training is not a simple cultural relic. The martial arts are as much focused on product—skills development—as they are on process—the constellation of cultural trappings that surround the arts. As "practical arts," we would expect that the retention of kaho reflects a functional appreciation of the method as a pedagogical tool.

A) Pedagog

We may posit that *kaho* must be an extremely flexible instructional tool to survive in the modern dojo. In the first place, we must remind ourselves that martial arts study is voluntary. While school children in Japan are still required to take judo or kendo in school, further training is a result of individual initiative. And in the West, martial arts training halls fall squarely within the category of "voluntary organizations." Participation presupposes a willingness to study, often because of some perceived benefit. But the motivations for training are as varied as the trainees themselves, and so may be the levels of ability. This mandates a flexible technique for teaching that may be one element in ensuring the continuing importance of kaho.

Some students approach the martial arts as exotic forms of exercise. Those of us who have trained in these arts for any length of time, after inventorying the bruises, broken bones, etc. involved may wonder whether there are other activities that create less wear and tear, but it remains that many consider martial arts training a calisthenic activity.

In the West, the allure of fighting skills development often forms a part in martial arts marketing. We might note in passing that this idea is not seriously entertained in Japan. But for Westerners, the hint of Asian mystery and the promise of arcane mastery embodied in every cheap B-grade martial arts movie keeps this questionable self-defense motivation alive. Other students are attracted by the vague yet comfortably exotic ideological trappings of some martial arts systems. They seek a sort of experiential transcendence in their training.

All of which suggests that the student body of a typical martial arts dojo is extremely heterogeneous in terms of personal motivation and athletic ability. This complicates issues relating to "practical" activities such as sparring, where questions of size, strength, endurance, willingness to experience pain, etc. are highly variable. The need for a mechanism for imparting the fundamentals of a particular system, while not introducing unwanted or undue stress on trainees, may well account for an emphasis on kata in training. We note that the more competitive modern forms of the martial arts—that is, those systems that rigidly segregate trainees into classes of higher and lower competencies and are composed of aggressive personalities—are ones that have drifted away from a heavy reliance on *kaho* as an instructional method.

In addition, we must also remember that the pace of this process of mastery is determined by the individual pupil's aptitude. Martial arts training displays no temporal structure to the training cycle, and entering cohorts are quickly eroded by the notoriously high drop-out rates within dojos. In addition, training may be considered a "spiral" rather than lineal process: trainees continue to refine even the most elemental skills throughout their training careers. Differing physical capacities, levels of emotional maturity, and psychological factors create varying dynamics for each student. Any experienced martial arts instructor knows that there are fairly consistent patterns in aggregate learning, but that each student brings a unique set of strengths and weaknesses to the process. The cyclical nature of training using kata thus permits general progression to take place while at the same time permitting individual focus on specific deficiencies.

Kata practice is also an activity that can be engaged in alone or by groups of students of various age levels or competencies—a key point stressed by modernizers such as Funakoshi Gichin (1868-1957). As such, it is a technique ideally suited to maximizing teachability among heterogeneous populations, an important consideration when we consider the activity's voluntary nature and its existence within a market context.

B) Practicality

There are also basic issues relating to "crowd control" and safety that recommend *kaho*. It was considered essential in the *ko-bujutsu*, the old systems of Japan, which are heavily weapons oriented. In addition to the cultural influences cited earlier, the extreme lethality of edged weapons introduces complications in the teaching method: training must be as realistic as possible, but not induce casualties among the trainees. The mechanics of controlling a class of novices wielding razor sharp or heavy wooden weapons suggests that *kaho* permitted a replication of successful combat techniques in a choreographed manner.

A room full of students using a slashing weapon like the Japanese sword (*katana*), for instance, provides some real and very serious immediate practical considerations. The wind up and finish embodied in techniques using a three-foot sword create a zone of danger around each swordsman. Trainees need to learn critical issues regarding distance and safe management of the weapon. They need to learn to wield their weapons well and to avoid those of their fellow students. This is not a trivial concern. Note that the sorts of weapons typically used in the martial arts are characteristic of individual, heroic combat styles. The greater the density of fighters in one spot, the higher the likelihood of a literal type of collateral damage. Armies that utilize mass formations tend to emphasize thrusting attacks, since they focus danger to the front and toward the enemy and minimize the possibility of self-inflicted wounds. The techniques developed for the Roman legionnaire's gladius, the Zulu impi's assegai, and the Greek hoplite's spears and swords all support this observation. Japan's weapons systems, forged in a different age, provide unique problems for group practice.

Viewed from this perspective, we can understand kaho's practical aspect as something driven by the need to create a pattern of behavior that protects students from themselves and each other, as well as one that provides an environment in which instructions for complex skills can be communicated, despite the emotional overlay of excitement, fear, and effort.

As mentioned before, kata are also models of success. They are thought to embody lessons learned by past masters. Like all cultural learning, they serve as a type of compacted, highly condensed information stream that holds multiple lessons for practitioners. Thus, kata can be used to teach the rudiments of a system, to refine growing skill, and also to reveal more subtle applications (bunkai) to advanced practitioners.

C) Ideas and Emotions

In more modern martial arts forms, the emphasis on kata is also driven by ideological factors that seek to create a mind-set that is not solely focused on combat. In this sense, katas form an integral part of the "moving Zen" experience many people seek in martial arts training—a physically and mentally engaging activity that generates a sense of intrinsic self-satisfaction consistent with the psychological concept of "flow" (see Csikszentmihalyi, 1975, 1990).

The discipline needed to diligently practice and master kata may also serve as a mechanism to test the commitment to an art. Dojos abound with stories of enthusiastic novices whose commitment fades quickly and whose numbers evaporate over time. There may be an element of planning in this phenomenon: martial arts teachers wish to test the commitment and the mettle of potential students—their attitude as much as their aptitude—and kata practice can serve as en excellent vehicle to do so.

There is also an additional ritual and aesthetic quality to kata performance. The stereotyped movements replicated through kata performance may be understood to be doing a number of things: they serve as a public statement of adherence to a particular martial arts style, they are a visible indicator of an individual's acquisition of skill, they provide the opportunity to experience a "flow" experience directly linked to the mystical-religious aspects of the martial arts that attract so many Westerners, and, to the extent that performance is skillful, it draws both observers and performers into an aesthetic community that identifies and reaffirms basic underlying systemic principles.

Katas have both cultural and technical influences, and are practices for form and function. Mr. Giles Hopkins illustrates a Goju-ryu solo form and its application from the Saifa kata. *Photographs courtesy of G. Hopkins.*

Conclusion

Westerners tend to view *kaho* as a cultural relic. Its persistence as a teaching tool in the Japanese martial tradition, however, may suggest that there is a functionality present in the method that is often overlooked. As with most sociological phenomena, there is a complex network of influences at play here.

The tradition of *kaho* is shaped by two major categories of influences: the cultural and the technical. Cultural patterns inherent in East Asian society during the formative period of martial arts development certainly account for some aspects of these systems: clothing, terminology, etiquette, and even kata practice. This is not, however, the only element at play here.

The fighting systems' overwhelmingly "practical" nature suggests that more mundane factors may be at play. We have identified pedagogical issues that support a continued utilization of *kaho*, practical considerations that are created by the nature of the human/weapon interface, and more psychological aspects that serve to answer more complex emotional needs of practitioners. It is hoped that the exercise, like the practice of kata itself, assists in revealing the sophisticated and complex nature of these martial systems.

BIBLIOGRAPHY

Budden, P. (2000). *Looking at a far mountain: A study of kendo kata*. Rutland, VT: Tuttle Publishing.

Craig, D. (1999). *The heart of kendo*. Boston: Shambhala.

Csikszentmihalyi, M. (1990). *Flow: The psychology of optimal experience*. New York: Harper and Row.

Csikszentmihalyi, M. (1975). *Beyond boredom and anxiety: The experience of play and work in games*. San Francisco, CA: Josey-Bass.

Donohue, J. (1991). The dimensions of discipleship: Organizational paradigm, mystical transmission, and vested interest in the Japanese martial tradition. *Ethnos*, 55, 1-2.

Friday, K., with Humitake, S. (1997). *Legacies of the sword: The Kashima Shinryu and samurai martial culture*. Honolulu: University of Hawaii Press.

Friday, K. (1995). Kabala in motion: Kata and pattern practice in traditional bugei. *Journal of Asian Martial Arts*, 4(4), 27-39.

Hanson, V. (1989). *The western way of war: Infantry battle in classical Greece*. Berkeley, CA: University of California Press.

Hsu, F. (1975). *Iemoto: The heart of Japan*. Cambridge: Belknap Press.

Hurst, G. (1998). *Armed martial arts of Japan: Swordsmanship and archery*. New Haven, CT: Yale University Press.

Inoue Y. (2002a). A philosophical look at kata. *Kendo World, 1*(2), 34-38.

Inoue Y. (2002b). The philosophy of kata: Part 2. *Kendo World, 1*(3), 59-69.

Kawaishi, M. (1982). *The complete 7 katas of judo*. Woodstock, NY: Overlook Press.

Kano, J. (1986). *Kodokan judo*. Tokyo: Kodansha International.

King, W. (1993). *Zen and the way of the sword: Arming the samurai psyche*. Oxford: Oxford University Press.

Lee, B. (1975). *The Tao of Jeet Kun Do*. Burbank, CA: Ohara Publishing.

Leggett, T. (1978). *Zen and the ways*. Rutland, VT: Charles E. Tuttle Co.

Morris, D. (1965). *The washing of the spears*. New York: Simon and Schuster.

Nakane, C. (1970). *Japanese society*. Berkeley, CA: University of California Press.

Onuma, H., with De Prospero, D., and De Prospero, J. (1993). *Kyudo: The essence and practice of Japanese archery*. Tokyo: Kodansha International.

Otaki, T., and Draeger, D. (1983). *Judo formal techniques: A complete guide to Kodokan Randori no Kata*. Rutland, VT: Charles E. Tuttle Co.

Suzuki, D. (1959). *Zen and Japanese culture*. Princeton, NJ: Princeton University Press.

Warner, G., and Draeger, D. (1982). *Japanese swordsmanship: Theory and practice*. Tokyo: Weatherhill.

chapter 10

Progressive Instruction Inherent in Standardized Form Practice Using Iaido for Illustration

by Kim Taylor, M.Sc.

Introduction

Instruction through kata training has formed an important part of training in many classical and modern Japanese martial systems. Kata training has sometimes been criticized, especially by contemporary Western martial artists as overly formal, rigid, and lacking in realism. But its use over the centuries suggests that, while no means the only form of training, kata practice has important things to impart.

This chapter explores the ways in which the practice of a specific kata, the Omori-ryu of the Muso Jikiden Eishin-ryu, can assist in the development of significant basic skills. It maintains that this training regimen can significantly help martial artists develop a solid foundation in terms of correct stance and the generation of power through the hips. The author notes that he believes that *iaido* (the art of drawing and cutting in one motion with the sword) is one of the best places for a martial arts student to concentrate on such things as posture, hip control, and the transfer of power. This is because iaido can be considered a "closed" art, one that is done by practice designed to lead the trainee to the replication of an ideal form. This is in contrast to an "open" art which involves much more variation in performance due to the presence of another person. Good examples of closed and open Western sports would be gymnastics as compared to tennis. Certainly the modern contest forms of martial arts exhibit heavily "open" characteristics as well. In Japanese swordsmanship, iaido has maintained a "closed" structure, while kendo is an example of an "open" form due to its emphasis on competition (*shiai*).

A secondary purpose for this chapter it to make explicit what is often implicit in kata training. In traditional systems, students are not usually told what they are learning in each kata. There is an assumption that skill will develop naturally with practice and that this developing insight will infuse all elements of training over time. This is a function of cultural patterns that emphasize hierarchy and rote learning, with little discussion of method and purpose. While traditional training has much to recommend it, more focused examination of effective elements in martial arts instruction can help improve that instruction.

> **GUIDE — Eleven Katas of Omori-ryu used to demonstrate progressive instruction**
> 1. *Mae*: front
> 2. *Migi*: right
> 3. *Hidari*: left
> 4. *Ushiro*: rear
> 5. *Yae gaki*: double-defense
> 6. *Uke nagashi*: receive/deflect
> 7. *Kaeshaku*: assistant
> 8. *Tsuke komi*: close range
> 9. *Tsuke kage*: moon shadow
> 10. *Oi kaze*: chasing the wind
> 11. *Nuki uchi*: draw cut

Lessons from the Omori-ryu of the Muso Jikiden Eishin-ryu

The purpose of this chapter is to provide an idea of the sort of cascading instruction that one can get through practice of a set of *kata* (pre-arranged, patterned movements). These lessons are often deeply embedded in the process of practice and are sometimes hard to acknowledge. In addition, the traditional approach to learning kata—emulation rather than discussion—can serve to sometimes hinder realization as well. Kata training in many martial arts forms involves similar features—standardization of technique, emphasis on proper form, sequence, timing, and an emphasis on experiential versus theoretical learning.

In this case we will be using *iaido* kata as a specific example. We will discuss the Omori-ryu set of the Muso Jikiden Eishin-ryu, a fairly well-known sword drawing school which was founded several hundred years ago and organized into its current form by Oe Masamichi (1852-1927) in the early 20th century. The Omori-ryu is the first set of kata taught in the Muso Jikiden Eishin-ryu and is thus intended to demonstrate the fundamentals of practice.

The very first kata that a student will learn in Omori-ryu is *Mae* (moving to the front) which is quite simple, consisting of a horizontal and then a vertical cut. Mae is the base, the root, the original kata for this set and to the educated eye its performance will reveal the performer's depth of knowledge.

Ten more kata follow, many of which are structured more or less on the same pattern of a horizontal and then vertical cut. There is, however, a developmental sequence to the series: in each, some basic principles of movement are repeated while something new is added as well. The student is expected to learn the new information and then to apply it back to Mae the next time he performs the kata.

Like many highly complex physical skills involving mental and physical integration, there are many things being taught and being learned in kata. For now we can concentrate on a few points for illustration. The main focus in this discussion will be on the use of the hips to provide power from the ground through to the attacking part of the sword. We will doubtless touch on other, more specific aspects of iaido, but posture and the use of the hips is key to all Japanese martial arts so this will provide an insight into the process of learning kata that will be understood by a wide audience.

As should be blindingly obvious, what follows is my particular understanding of iaido, and my particular understanding of the underlying principles. It is not intended to be definitive, since varying instructors and practitioners can have differing insights.

INSIGHT
With the first four kata described below, we will establish a good posture and great stability in the hips, while also learning how to project directly to the target from any starting angle.

#1 – MAE (Defending to the Front)

First, a quick description of the kata.

This is a horizontal cut to the front, followed by a vertical finishing cut, *chiburi* (shaking off the blood) and *noto* (putting the blade in the scabbard). The photos should provide a good idea of the movements.

This first kata moves straight forward. We must work out how to drive power from the hips directly forward into the opponent as a first principle. To do that, we emphasize moving from the center of the body, the center of balance at the *tanden*, which is a point about two fingers below the navel, and midway through the body. You can find the spot by laying yourself over a railing, where you balance in any direction (arms and legs on opposite sides, arm and leg on one side or the other, and sitting upright with your legs on either side will likely give you a pretty good idea.)

A good exercise to find out how to move from the *tanden*, and which muscles are involved, is to use a *jo* (4 foot staff) with a partner. The partner stands in front and provides resistance to your *tanden* through the staff, while you rise and step forward.

Draw and Cut

This movement must come from the center, so the hands are positioned in such a way that they move from the center in and forward with the draw. When grasping the handle, the hands both travel upward together, the left hand reaches the hilt first, then the right. Grasp the hilt from below, not on top, which keeps the elbows down, closer to the *tanden*.

The cut must have power from the hips. The hips do not move up then down during the move, they rise to the proper height and are driven forward during the cut. The cut and the foot stamp are timed together and the level motion of the hips prevents a wavy motion of the tip on the cut.

At the finish of the cut, the knuckles should be just below the level of the right shoulder. The tip should be just below parallel with the floor. The horizontal cut is given power by uniting the tip with the hips through the shoulders and torso, this is done by keeping the shoulders down, armpits tight, and closing the scapula at the bottom, while opening the chest.

Vertical Strike

On the next move, the shoulders and arms must be relaxed, while the hips retain their power. The blade moves around and up while the left hand moves from the center of the body directly upward to grasp the hilt. The tip is brought up and over at the same time as the hips are driven forward and the cut is stabilized with the little fingers, armpits, and stomach through the part of the arc where it would be cutting.

Keeping the hips under the shoulders and maintaining an upright posture is very important to the ability to drop your weight into the cutting edge of the sword, the closer your *tanden* is to being under the cut, the more weight you can drop into it. Think about a ladder with hooks on the top, if you lean it up against a wall you aren't putting much pressure downward on the wall at all, but if you hook it over the top of the wall so that the ladder is vertical, you get maximum pressure. The sword is the hook, and your body is the ladder. The cut is the wall.

Shaking Off the Blood

front

side

Sheathing

front

side

Lessons Learned: In this kata we have found our *tanden*, learned how to move from there, and how to unite the trio of sword tip, hips and floor. On the theory that we can't learn everything all at once, we will leave Mae now and move on to the next kata so that we can learn something new.

#2 – MIGI (Defending to the Right)

The opponent is seated to your left. He begins to rise up and draw. You turn 90 degrees to the left and cut horizontally across his chest, raise the blade as in #1 Mae, and cut down from his head to his groin. The *chiburi*, foot change, and sheathing are as for Mae, but the opposite foot is forward throughout the movement.

Draw and Cut Right

This technique "is" frontward (*Mae*), only performed toward an opponent to the left. We must get the same direct movement toward the opponent as we do in Mae, but while turning. To do this, we have to envision a straight line from our right hand, through the hilt, to the center of the opponent. Our right hand moves along this line as we attack. To rise and turn at the same time, we need to do some fairly complex hip movements and weight shifting.

First, move the right knee toward the opponent, to touch the left knee. This makes sure we don't actually move backward as we turn, but it also puts our right knee in the center of our body as we're sitting. Now as soon as we start to lift the hips, straight forward from our original position, our weight shifts onto the right knee. By pulling back on the left hip, and driving into the right hip, our body spins naturally to the left. At the same time we start to feel the power move from the *tanden* toward the opponent as we draw the blade along that straight line. The back foot plants to stop the turn as we cut horizontally.

None of this works if we throw our heads forward to turn. If that happens, we will spin outward and off balance as our heads act like eccentric weights on the side of a spinning axle. Just as we don't turn right or left as we walk, or stand by throwing our heads and chests around first, we don't lean forward to defend to the right (#2 Migi).

Lessons Learned: With the second kata we have learned more hip and weight shifting, reinforced the feeling of attacking directly into the center of the opponent, and become much more aware of our right hip as we drive it around and forward. We have also learned how to cut with the legs changed, which means we are rooted into the ground differently, which helps us to further understand what's happening in the hips.

Reflection: What we take back into #1 Mae: We now have a better awareness of our right hip (as the right hand brushes by it and we imagine it driving toward the opponent), we know not to throw our heads forward as we rise to defend to the front (Mae) (just as we can't when defending right, #2 Migi), and we likely have a stronger pull of the scabbard as we must use our left hand more to clear the tip of the blade out of the scabbard.

#3 – **HIDARI** (Defending to the Left)

Draw and Cut Left
This kata turns to face an opponent to the right side.

Here is a slightly different way to visualize our turn, since a straight line from the right hand to the opponent will leave the sword behind. We need to move the left knee to the right, rise and turn much like we did attacking right (Migi), shifting the weight onto the left knee and pulling back the right hip. In this case though, the left hand moves past our centerline and picks up the hilt, moving it into the right hand on its way directly toward the target.

As we reach the position where we hit the target, the hips are rotating past that target, or are not doing anything at all. Here we need to rotate the hips to square, and then drive the left hip back into the left foot to root it as we cut horizontally. This is the first time that we've had to change the rotation of the hips in order to stabilize them before we cut. It's also the first time that we've changed the movement of the sword from left hand to right to left again on the vertical cut.

Lessons Learned: With attacking right and left (#2 Migi and #3 Hidari) we are starting to get a much better feeling of driving the hilt toward the opponent, while keeping the hip strong and the posture erect. We have also developed a feel for both sides of the hip, and how they can be used in combination with the *tanden* to create a strong base for the cuts. The importance of the rear foot to the cut, and a more efficient, smooth transfer of power from hand to hand has been demonstrated.

Reflection: The foot position and the stability of the hips should be much better now when defending toward the front (#1 Mae).

#4 – USHIRO (Defending to the Rear)

The opponent is seated to your rear. He begins to rise up and draw. In one smooth movement, you turn 180° to the left and cut horizontally across his chest, raising the blade as in #1 Mae (front), and cut down from his head to his groin. The *chiburi*, foot change, and sheathing are as for Mae but the opposite foot is forward throughout the movement.

Draw and Cut Behind

front ‹

side ‹

This kata, Mae to the rear, is an excellent reinforcement of the skills we've learned so far in turning, since you turn 180°, any lean of the head or the torso will throw you off balance. The right knee shifting to the left and in front of the left knee will allow you to shift your weight as you did in defending right and left (Migi and Hidari), so that you can turn.

The new problem here is that your hands cannot "see" the opponent, so it's hard to draw straight toward him. You would have to draw through your own body, so we must deal with the turn. In order to draw straight toward the target, we must know our hand has cleared the left hip. Here is where the eyes become important. Without straining the neck, if we turn our eyes, then our head as we rise until we can see the target and are in position to cut directly. The right hand is actually moving slightly away from the opponent, so as we line up to draw at him we must switch from a right hand movement to a very strong left hand movement to clear the scabbard from the blade as we turn. Dealing with this turn means a great deal of attention to our posture and to keeping the hips working without putting tension in the upper body and especially not in the shoulders.

Lessons Learned: We have now learned how to deal with our non-seeing right hand, and with an opponent we can't see, we've learned the importance of catching the opponent with our eyes and using that motion to begin our turn and cut.

Reflection:

We can now defend to the front (*Mae*) with good posture, great stability in the hips, to an opponent at any position around us.

> **INSIGHT**
> The next kata requires the swordsman to learn to take the principles in the first four kata and become more mobile, with a second series of attack and defense.

#5 – *YAE GAKI* ("Double Fence" Defense)

The opponent is seated in the frontal defense (*Mae*). As he starts to rise, you draw and cut as in Mae, but he shuttles backward out of range. You step forward with the left foot as you cut down from his head to his groin. Perform "double fence defense" and sheathing, drawing the left foot back to the right knee. At this point, the attacker strikes at your right knee so you draw and block this attack while stepping back with the left foot. Take the left knee to the right foot, bring the blade around and over your head, and cut down almost to the floor as you shift the right foot forward to the square positions again. Raise the tip out of the attacker, and then perform chiburi and sheathing as in #1 Mae.

This is Mae with a second engagement. The main feature of this kata is the second attack and defense, demonstrating the importance of a "relaxed alertness" (*zanshin*), and that the kata is never really "over" until you are back home. There are several new lessons here about posture as well.

Draw and Cut #1

front ‹

side ‹

On the first horizontal cut, the opponent has squirmed backward to avoid being cut, so you must chase him down. You do this by stepping forward with the left foot and cutting as you sink back down on your knee.

The key bit of instruction for this kata is here, as you plant the left foot on the first cut. To move forward smoothly you will take the weight off of the left knee, now the movement is smooth and with a natural arc of the hips.

Finishing Cut #1

Don't slam the left knee into the ground as you perform the vertical cut downward. Stop half an inch above the ground and then lower it the rest of the way. At this point your position is the same as when you finish #2 Migi.

Shaking Off Blood to the Side

This is the first time we encounter Shaking Off Blood to the Side (*yoko chiburi*), which is the most common chiburi in the school. Release the handle with the left hand as you move the sword very slightly forward with the right. The left hand moves to the scabbard's opening, pulling the scabbard into the belt at the left side. Moving the blade as a whole, not leaving the tip behind, snap the sword directly out to the right side so that it stops about 20 cm to the right of the right knee. The tip points directly forward and is just slightly below the level of the blade at the guard. The blade is flat with the edge pointing out from your body.

Usually, when we do *chiburi* we forget to keep the hips alive, and by now all our weight is on our downed knee. This sets us up for some lurches and grunts as we rise. What happens next in this kata teaches us not to be so careless.

Sheathing the Sword #1

From this position, move the open end of the scabbard to the center and bring the back of the blade directly over to perform the sheathing. Draw the sword out and place it into the scabbard as in Mae. As you slide the sword into the scabbard, maintain "relaxed awareness" and pull the left foot back and in toward the right ankle so that the left heel is near the anklebone. Again, we must use the hip to do this movement. We can't rock our body back until there is no weight on the foot and then pull the foot back. If we are attacked while doing that, we are helpless. At any point along this foot pulling movement we must be able to rise into a standing position. To do this, we must move the foot back with some weight on it, and use the hip to shift the foot. Now we can respond if necessary, and it turns out to be necessary.

Draw and Cut #2 (Shin Guard)

front

side

Just before you position to sheath the sword, the opponent manages to cut with his sword toward the outside of your right knee. Draw the sword out until 1" is left in the scabbard as you rise straight up. With a strong pull-back on the scabbard, clear the tip and swing it down in front of your right foot to stop about 8" in front and 4" to the right of your toes. Turn the back of the sword toward your leg as you block the opponent's blade, thus saving your leg from damage if the blade is knocked back again into your shin.

As you swing the blade down, the left foot is thrust straight back so that a right stance is taken. Make sure that it is a strong stance and that the hips are stable so that the block will be solid. The hips are usually turned to a half forward position (*hanmi*) at this block and if they are loose, your block will not hold. The best way to get to this position is to think of thrusting the left heel outward from your center, and turn the toes as close as possible toward the opponent without losing the power in the right arm.

Move the left knee down to the right ankle as you bring the sword around the left side of your body and raise it above your head. Shift the right foot forward to the proper position as you do a dropping cut into the opponent's body as he lies on the ground. It's important to move under the sword with your hips rather than pulling the sword back and releasing the pressure on the opponent. At the finish of the cut, the legs must be square at the knees and the back straight. All this is best done by working from the hips, driving them down under the sword and toward the opponent.

Finishing Cut #2

To avoid dropping the hips and raising them again, you must also stretch the hips upward (keep the left leg extended downward) when setting the left knee on the ground. The importance of an upward posture is reinforced here.

At this point, finish the kata as done for Mae.

Shaking Off Blood #2

Sheathing Sword #2

Lessons Learned: First, as the initial horizontal cut is made, the rear foot is usually mentioned. Here is where the concept of lifting the rear knee just clear of the ground on the initial cut is introduced. This is to enable the drive forward into the full step before the vertical cut to be made smoothly and without hesitation. It also provides a much stronger and more stable hip for the horizontal cut and so should be tried in the first four kata. Of course once it is, the problem of how to slide forward for the vertical cut is met. It is in working out how to drive the rear foot into the ground while still being able to slide forward on the cut that the student learns even more about the hip girdle and how it works. Being able to do all that smoothly, without bouncing up and down or rocking back and forth is a complex skill that must be approached systematically, as we have done here.

The block after the second attack is the introduction of a standing posture where we need to be as precise with the hip position as we do on our knees. The left foot is driven back and the heel turned outward in order to make a strong posture. If the foot is moved carelessly, the hip is likely to be loose and the block will fail. The drive back downward with the left knee for the final cut is also done from the hips.

All this movement gives ample opportunity to practice control of the hips so that the body is smooth, and the cuts and blocks accurate.

The final downward cut is a great check on the torso, with any sort of lean forward, the student will drive his blade into the floor. A straight posture means that the blade stops an inch from disaster.

A balance of power between the feet at all times is key to this kata. We must not rock the body from foot to foot if we are to be prepared to move quickly in any direction. With two knees, a knee and a foot or two feet on the floor, we must be ready to move without hesitation and preparation.

Reflection: At this point, if you are working through this chapter, try to take the first draw and cut back to Mae. Do the horizontal cut with the left knee unweighted. Now, without dropping your weight back onto the knee to lurch forward, do the vertical cut with a surge forward of the hips. It will seem impossible to do, but can be done if you maintain pressure on the hips forward and simply pop the right foot off the floor. Remember to move from the hips, not the left foot or all sorts of unwanted things might happen.

> **INSIGHT**
> In the next three kata we learn how to drop our weight into the cut and to deal with our knees and ankles being free to move. Up to now the body has been stable through the hips because we've been kneeling on the floor. Now we must stand up.

#6 – UKE NAGASHI (Receive and Deflect)

In this kata, the attacker moves to us from the left side and cuts down once toward our head. As he begins to cut, we draw the blade horizontally forward while stepping forward with the left foot. He now lifts the blade and cuts again towards our head. Raise the blade and twist to the left to block the strike. To do this, move the right foot over so that you are now facing the attacker.

Now, turn the left foot on the spot and step up to it with the right foot as you raise the sword and cut down on the opponent with a strong hip drop. Move the left foot back along the opponent's original attack line as you move the hilt over to the left front and place the tip over the right knee. Change the right hand grip and then let the tip swing down and up again as you move the back ridge of the sword to the left hand. Draw the back ridge of the blade out and put the point into the scabbard's opening, then replace the blade, dropping down onto the left knee while returning back to the original position. The right hand is reversed to its usual position now, so when you finish sheathing you can change to the usual right hand grip and then stand up and move back as in Mae.

Draw and Cut

As you notice the opponent starting to attack, surge forward to avoid his cut by rising onto your right knee and stepping forward with your left foot. At the same time draw the blade horizontally forward. The lesson here should be obvious, you must move your hips out of the way of a cut, rather than just ducking. If you simply rock forward the opponent will still cut into your lower back. Move forward from the hips and take the left foot out of the way and he can slam his sword into the floor without hitting you.

In a fast move, the opponent now raises the sword quickly and cuts down once more. To block this cut, step forward with the right foot to a position where your body is lined up facing the opponent, and raise the blade to take the cut on the area just in front of your sword guard, held horizontally above and in front of your head.

The left foot is still twisted, so you had better have a solid right foot position to receive the cut or your left knee will suffer. The body position has to take a full force blow and transfer the power through your center and down into your right foot. The arm position, hip position, and leg positions are examined carefully here. Lines of force moving from sword to ground are clearly seen now, and when one moves back to Mae, the lines from the blade tip to the left foot are also a bit more clear.

Finishing Cut

After a definite brief stop at the block position, the sword is turned through raising movement (*furi kaburi*) and brought down in a one handed downward cut toward the opponent's exposed neck (*kiri otoshi*) as he leans forward to make his second cut. This cut is made as the left foot is raised, turned to face the opponent, and brought down again. As the cut is made and the left hand is brought to the hilt, the right foot is brought up beside the left. The cut finishes with the blade in a horizontal position, the feet together, the knees bent and the hips lowered.

This is the first cut we've performed that relies almost entirely on dropping the hips rather than on a braced rear leg. Instead of being weak as it might at first seem, the cut is surprisingly strong if we can connect the sword through our armpits to the hips. While we have little push from the leg muscles, we have the greatest amount of weight under the sword that we will ever have. This gives us a real feel for dropping our weight into a cut rather than muscling it over.

Wiping Off Blood

The next movement represents wiping the blood off the blade. Maintaining "relaxed awareness" (*zanshin*), the left foot is pulled back to your left rear from where you are currently facing to establish a position called *karuma*. The hips are turned off of square and the left heel is placed down onto the floor. The weight is evenly distributed on both feet. At the same time as the left foot is moved, the hands are moved to the left so that the tip of the blade is drawn straight back to finish 1 to 2 inches above the right knee. The blade is flat and the edge points away from the body. At this point, we would take a cloth and wipe the blade.

Parry Block

This hip position is similar in feel to the "double fence" (*Yae Gaki*) blocking position, reinforcing that lesson. As the blade is placed into the scabbard, the hips are rotated to the original forward position, which will be very painful or upsetting if we haven't placed our feet in the right position to begin with.

Sheathing the Sword

Lessons Learned:

We have mentioned the lessons above: the hip surge to avoid a strike, the lines of force from rear foot to the area just in front of your sword guard (*tsuba moto*) on the block, and the very powerful dropping of the weight into the cut. We have learned to cut powerfully while standing without dropping back onto our knee. The hips are key. The joints above and below them must be controlled, tightened and loosened as needed in order to make the sword cut as we want it to.

Reflection:

We are now expanding our feeling for our hips throughout our body and even into the sword and the ground. We are now prepared to go back to #1 Mae with a new appreciation of how to "cut from the hips" and how to get some real power into the sword. Speed and muscle are hopefully being replaced with power and weight.

#7 – KAESHAKU (Assistant)

This technique is different than those described previously. It is not a response to an attack by an enemy but is the method of assisting someone to commit suicide. The *kaeshaku* is the person designated to cut through the neck of the person who has just disemboweled himself. This is necessary, since a person with this type of stomach wound can survive for a long time in a great deal of pain.

Draw and Cut

front

side

Draw the blade out horizontally behind the back of the person performing suicide as you move the right foot forward slightly. Lift the sword tip over your head as you pull the right foot back into a left half stance (*hanmi*) position with the right elbow bent to 90 degrees, the forearm held vertically, and the blade at the same angle as the scabbard. At the appropriate moment, cut down one-handed to the neck, the left hand joining in time to prevent the tip from cutting through the skin at the throat. The position is a right half stance (*hanmi* or *karuma*) posture. Move the blade to the chiburi position as in the previous #6 Uke Nagashi, reverse the right hand grip, and then quietly sheath the sword.

Blood Wiping and Sheathing

front

Lessons Learned: The physical lessons in this kata are not as important as the psychological lessons, but I won't go into that here other than to ask a simple question. Why is it that this kata is placed here in the school? This is the seventh (yes the *shichi* or "death" position) kata in the very first set of things you learn. In fact, if you consider the first four katas to be the same one (Mae from four different directions) than this is the fourth (*shi* or, again, "death") kata. Why so soon? What do we need to learn from so cold-bloodedly taking a life, what is so important to know, this early in our education?

Physically of course, we continue to learn. The movements in this kata are without ill-feeling toward the one we are to cut; there is no enemy present, so we must move smoothly, quietly, and without distracting the other person present. This means that we need great control of our hips and tremendous leg strength as well as a very delicate touch on the blade. We are learning to separate the strong actions of the cut from the softer actions of moving the blade between the cuts.

The cut is also unusual, starting much lower than we are used to, and stopping so abruptly, all the power being focused between the back and front of the spine in the neck. In fact the only place in the entire kata where there is any power shown is in those few inches of cut. There has to be a very strong connection between hips and feet, and no tension in the shoulders at all for this to be done.

Reflection: Psychologically, our Mae should now be much more solemn and weighty, physically we should be moving the sword and ourselves with grace and control in the times between the cuts, while instantly applying tremendous power from the floor to the tip when needed.

#8 – *TSUKE KOMI* (For an Opening at Close Range)

The opponent walks toward you, intending to cut you down. Move forward and draw with *go ho nuki* (like pulling a radish from the ground) toward him, the right knee up as in the draw and cut of Mae. As he cuts down toward your head, stand up, move the blade up in a receive and deflect block (*Uke Nagashi*), and pull the right foot back. Immediately after his tip swings down past your nose, step forward and cut down from his forehead to his neck. The left foot moves up beside the right as you cut. Move forward once more with the right foot and the left following to cut from forehead to groin. Step back with the right foot and raise the blade to the upper stance (*jodan gamae*) position in to check the opponent. Move the blade over in a cutting motion as you sink down onto the right knee. Hold the handle with a reverse grip of the right hand, turn the blade over and wipe it using the left hand, pulling the blade's back ridge along the left palm. Sheath the sword, stand up, and then move back to the original position.

Draw and Cut

front

side

As you make the first motion to draw the blade you must cause your opponent to hesitate, step short and then cut short (to where you now are). The technique relies on this and he won't be fooled unless you fully intend to continue your draw into "Mae" and cut across his stomach. When he does stop short, just out of range of your draw, and cuts down towards your head, you can stand up and back causing him to miss. You have been prepared to do this short sharp movement to a standing position by the kata you've done so far in the set. The instant movement back and upward is not a problem now.

The two vertical cuts are done with a feeling of dropping the hips into the blade tip, something we've already learned. However, the movement between the two cuts is of extreme importance. This must be done with an intent of pressing forward from the hips and threatening the opponent with the blade tip. We have only dented his forehead with the first cut which was made one-handed and very fast, so we must continue to keep him on his heels and moving backward. If we don't move from the hips, or if we bounce off his head into the next cut, he will recover and escape or attack. The surge forward with the hip from our feet together position must feel exactly like the surge forward from the formal sitting posture (*seiza*) into draw and cut as in #1 Mae. It can't come from the shoulders.

Finishing Cut

front ◄

side ◄

Step back with the right foot and raise the sword high, expecting to step in immediately to cut once more. As the opponent collapses, we have no need to cut, so we slowly perform the motion of a droping downward cut (*kiri otoshi*) and sink down onto the right knee, finish with the sword held just above horizontal with the handle at the height of the left knee. If we have moved back properly and have the hips under control, there won't be any wavering around of the upper body and arms. The sword will move precisely and strongly but not stiffly.

Shaking Off Blood

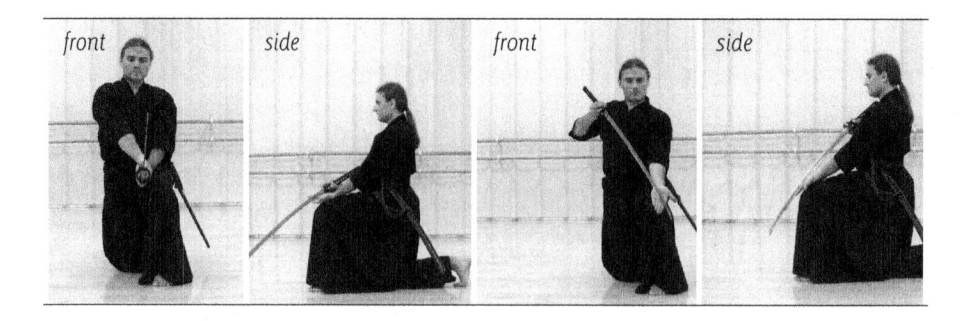

The right hand is turned over, the left wipes the blade, and the sword is put into the scabbard once more, this time without moving the left leg back. All this takes a long time and at the end of it, the entire body weight is usually on the right knee so standing up without lurching and grunting is impossible. The lesson of course is to maintain the body weight between the two feet and keep that right knee floating throughout the entire movement. A very difficult task and one that will build some good leg muscles. Perhaps there is something we can do with the hips to help here?

Sheathing

front *side*

Lessons Learned: Again we have mentioned them above, a powerful and convincing surge forward, followed by a sharp movement out of danger. What is new is the feeling of driving the opponent back relentlessly as we perform the vertical cuts.

Reflection: We must take this feeling of pounding forward into the opponent back into #1 Mae, especially in the timing between draw and cut, and finishing cut. On a basic level we can also apply this sort of driving threat to the movement of draw and cut.

> **INSIGHT**
> In the final three katas, we cut from various angles and levels (above and below) to complete our overall sphere of attack. We also return to the ground and to the most basic of sword movements in the final kata.

#9 – TSUKI KAGE (Moon Shadow)

Turn to the left 90 degrees and sit in formal posture (*seiza*). The opponent will walk toward you from the right side and strike in a vertical dropping cut (*kiri otoshi*). Grasp the blade and look at the opponent. Draw and turn on the left knee while sliding the right foot toward him. Rise off of the left knee and cut through the opponent's wrists from left to right. Move forward using a shortening and lengthening of the stance (*tsugi ashi*) and cut down from forehead to groin. Perform a large chiburi while standing, switch the feet, and then sheath the sword without sinking down on one knee.

This is of course our old friend #1 Mae, done toward an opponent to the right, but standing now instead of being on the floor with us. All the previous lessons apply, and it seems the only difference between #3 Defending Left and #9 Moon Shadow (*Hidari* and *Tsuke Kage*) is the angle of the horizontal cut.

Drawing Cut

There is, however, another lesson here, and that's in the turn and rise to a very low standing position on the opening cut. By turning and sliding the right foot out toward the opponent, we actually move toward him in such a way that he doesn't realize the combative distance has changed, and we can hit his wrists sooner than he believes we can. Another lesson here is how we rise up on this cut. If we simply stand up, we will move our heads into the attacking cut, so we must, instead, drive the left heel backward and down into the ground while keeping the hips at roughly the same height as when we are formally sitting (*seiza*). This requires and allows a much longer stance which, incidentally, lets us put our right foot much closer to the opponent.

Finishing Cut

The chiburi and sheathing are identical to #1 Mae, except that you do not drop down to the knee, but remain standing instead. We stand up to respond to a standing opponent, and the next kata starts from standing, so we remain standing for sheathing here. This is a lesson in hip control in itself, since our training and instinct is to drop as we put the blade away.

Shaking Off Blood and Sheathing

Lessons Learned: We now can perform #1 Mae in any direction and to any height. We have also learned about "stealing distance," moving toward an opponent without him realizing we've closed the gap. This is quite different to the driving pressure we applied in the close range defense of #8 Tsuke Komi. It is performed to the rear side, as opposed to the front side of Tsuke Komi.

Reflection: The hip control and power of this kata, driven through the back leg, must be applied in #1 Mae. The feeling of stealing distance can also be applied to the movement of draw and cut.

#10 – OI KAZE (Chasing the Wind)

Remain standing at the original position facing the front. Your opponent is running directly away from you. He is moving backward, trying to get clearance to draw his sword.

Remain standing throughout the whole kata. Grasp the sword as you drop your hips and then push the guard to start the sword out of the scabbard. Starting with the right foot, take two normal steps, then five short-to-long steps as you draw the sword finishing with a horizontal draw and cut across the opponent's shoulders. Step forward with a shuffle step (*tsugi ashi*), the left foot approaches but does not come in front of the right as you raise the sword and then cut down with the right foot forward. Perform a large chiburi and sheathing while standing, and move back to the starting position.

Chasing the Wind, Drawing Cut

Yes, as you suspected, this is #1 Mae while running. To start, bend the knees as you lower the hips and grasp the handle, lean forward until you come unbalanced over your toes. Now take two long steps to catch your balance and to close the distance between you and your opponent. He doesn't have the room to draw so has to start moving backward, when he does you chase. Keep the distance close, but allow it to lengthen as you straighten your body up, driving your hips forward while drawing. When the sword just clears the scabbard (*saya banari*), draw and cut the opponent across the shoulders.

Bring the left foot up to the right as you raise the sword. Step forward with the right foot and cut downward (*kiri otoshi*) finishing with the blade horizontal.

Finishing Cut

Keep the hips at the same height throughout the kata. Move under the sword and keep the movement going forward as you do the final cut. It's important to keep driving forward with the hips to make sure opponent stays on his heels and backing up.

Shaking Off Blood and Sheathing

The shaking off blood and sheathing movements are as in #9 Moon Shadow.

Lessons Learned: The importance of doing a "samurai run" with the feet close to the ground, short steps and the hips lowered is brought home in this kata since at any moment you may have to stop and cut, or even reverse direction. The idea of a "stable gun platform" helps with this feeling. Imagine trying to hit something with very powerful cannon on a small boat, at long distances it can't be done because the platform is bouncing all over the place. That's why heavy battleships were invented, to provide a gun platform that was steady enough to hit a target miles away. The same thing is required for the sword. One can't hit the target if the hips are bouncing up and down or slopping around from side to side. Keep it smooth and controlled.

Reflection: The same idea of a stable hip translates back to #1 Mae of course. While it may not be immediately apparent that you are bouncing up and down when you're on your knees, after trying to run and having the knees and ankles flexing, it should be easier to feel that bouncing in our base kata.

#11 – *Nuki Uchi* (Draw and Cut)

Sit formally (*seiza*) once more facing forward. Your opponent is facing you as in #1 Mae. He attacks directly and quickly. As he starts to draw, you draw from the sitting position, lift the blade over the head while raising your hips then cut down, splitting the knees for power. Perform a small sideways chiburi, sheathing, and lower the hips again. Close the knees, return to the formal sitting posture, and put the hands back onto the lap.

Drawing and Finishing Cuts

Lessons Learned: Here we have the final test of what you've learned about your hips. The draw is done with a surge forward as we rise to the knees so that we slide forward about six inches and then cut as we drop the hips downward with the knee split. Weak hips and stiff shoulders will result in stabbing ourselves rather than cutting the opponent.

Reflection: Strong hips and relaxed shoulders are, as always, the key and of course this is what we take back to #1 Mae from this final kata which is the essence of iaido, a draw, directly into a final cut.

Shaking Off Blood and Sheathing

By the end of this series of kata the student has learned the fundamentals of swordwork, and most specifically has learned how to use the hips in an efficient and powerful manner. This will provide a powerful base for further instruction in the other levels and sets of practice.

Conclusions

This chapter presented an examination of how posture, hip control and the transfer of power from the ground to the tip of the sword is taught through a series of kata. The implicit lessons which are learned by studying the set in sequence have been partially examined with the hope that students who study in this way will look at their own practice and perhaps find similar insights. I hope that this examination of the Omori-ryu of Muso Jikiden Eishin-ryu has provided the reader with some idea of how a series of simple exercises can be used to teach and learn the basics, and to deepen that practice through various additional exercises which highlight different aspects of the skills.

ACKNOWLEDGMENT

I would like to thank Dennis Nikitenko and Nathan Bain for demonstrating the techniques.

index

aikido, 37, 64, 70-72, 74, 76, 79, 82, 84, 86, 89-90
All-Japan Kendo Federation, 86
appropriate behavior (giri), 5, 8-11, 13, 45, 62, 71, 73, 84, 93-94, 101, 110, 116
archery, 1, 39-40, 46, 49
artistic way (geido), 37-40, 47-51
basic movements (kihon), 31, 33, 71, 73, 92-93, 99, 101-102, 120, 151
blood oath (kappan), 45, 51
Bodhidharma, 1
body armor, 18, 82, 48
Buddhism, 1, 20, 56, 95
martial art (bugei), 17-18, 21-23, 40-41, 43, 45, 48-49, 55-63, 65 notes 1 and 9, 66 notes 15 and 18, 81-82, 88, 90, 99
martial methods (bujutsu), 17, 81-85, 87-91, 109-110, 115
certification of mastery, 23, 38, 42, 44-45, 61
certified complete transmission (menkyo kaiden), 45, 76
civilian marital art, 21, 80-81, 83, 107
competition (shiai), 18, 27-28, 63, 82, 88-90, 93, 120
Confucianism, 58-59, 92, 112
contest with other schools (taryu jiai), 47, 53 note 21
Csikszentmihalyi, Mihalyi, 8, 90
dan/kyu ranking, 23, 85, 92, 111-112
Daoism, 18, 95
devotion to an art, 50-51
discipleship (deshi), 22, 41, 44-46, 48, 84-85, 110-111
divine transmission, 19-20, 42
dojo altar (kamidana), 42
dojo storming (dojo arashi), 23

family headship system (iemoto), 37-39, 41-45, 47-49, 51 notes 2 and 4, 85, 111
"flowery swordplay" (kaho kenpo), 63
Funakoshi, Gichin, 1-2, 33-34, 115
Grotowski, Jerzy, 3
hakama (uniform skirt), 84
harmony (wa), 61, 69-71, 76-78
harmonious interaction (musubi), 70-71
Herrigel, Eugen, 1
hierarchy, 73, 96, 110, 113, 121
Hori, Victor, 58, 60
iaido, 82, 90, 120
imitating the master, 59-61, 71-72, 76, 110
indebtedness (on), 73, 78
Issai Chozan, 56
Itto-ryu, 24, 63, 84
Jikishinkage-ryu, 67 note 23
short staff (jodo), 70-71, 73-74, 76-77
judo, 18, 37, 49, 55, 64, 81-82, 84, 88-89, 91, 101-102, 110, 114
junior student (kyohai), 84, 110
jujutsu, 81-82, 102
jutsu, 17, 86
Kano, Jigoro, 81-82, 102
Kashima Shin-ryu, 84
kendo, 18, 37, 50, 55, 64, 82, 88-89, 93, 114, 120
Kumano Shrine, 45
Langer, Susanne, 31-32, 34-35
learning through the body, 5-6, 8, 48-49
martial applications (bunkai), 34, 57, 61, 86, 88, 93, 98, 116-117
martial art pledges (kishomon), 45
master teacher (shihan), 19, 25, 41, 45, 56
mental attitude (kokorogamae), 5, 8, 48, 116
mind-to-mind transmission (ishin-denshin),

56-58
Muso Jikiden Eishin-ryu, 109, 120-121, 151
Myerhoff, Barbara, 4
Nakanishi Chuta, 18
non-discursive symbolism, 27-28, 31-36
Ogyu Sorai, 62
Omori-ryu, 120-122, 151
performance, 2, 8-9, 13-14, 38, 52 note 9, 62, 88, 93, 99, 101, 107-110, 116-117, 120, 122
pattern practice (kata), 8-9, 21, 27, 31, 47, 49-50, 54-56, 58-64, 65 note 1, 66 note 15, 69, 71-72, 74-75, 87-88, 92-93, 107-118, 120-122, 151
"preserve-defend-separate" (shu-ha-ri), 24-25, 61, 99
progressive instruction, 120
school (ryuha), 16-17, 25, 37, 40-49, 52 note 10, 54-58, 60-64
secret teachings (hiden, okuden), 21, 41-46, 50, 53 note 15, 60, 64, 95
self-mastery, 6-7
senior student (sempai), 22, 24, 43, 74, 84, 94, 110, 112
Shaolin, 1
Shintoism, 19-20, 42, 45, 86, 95, 111
Shinto-ryu, 16, 63
shinai sword, 18, 67 note 23, 82
Shindo Musu-ryu, 22, 70, 79
Shotokan Karate, 27-29, 31, 33-34, 84, 110
sparring (kumite), 3, 9-10, 12, 22, 31, 55, 62-64, 77, 88, 93, 114
martial sport, 18, 22, 27, 80, 82-83, 88-90, 93, 107
student/teacher relationship, 7-8, 11, 18, 21-22, 24, 39, 41, 43-47, 49, 52 note 9, 53 note 15, 54, 56-57, 59-60, 62, 72-77, 84, 91-94, 96-97, 100-102, 110, 115-116, 121
Tenshin Shoden Katori Shinto-ryu, 83,
school text/scrolls, 42-44, 47-48, 50-51,

53 note 13, 56-57
Toda-ryu, 63
Tokugawa Ieyasu, 20, 47
Turner, Victor, 10, 13-14
Ueshiba, Morihei, 70, 86
verbal transmission (kuden), 44, 47, 53 note 13, 58
ritual, 4-5, 9-10, 14, 28, 31, 33, 38-43, 52 note 9, 55, 58-59, 71, 82, 84, 92, 110, 112, 116
wandering martial apprenticeship (musha shugyo), 23, 25, 62, 66 notes 17 and 18
written transmission (kudensho), 44
Yagyu Shinkage-ryu, 20, 41, 47, 63, 84
Zen, 1-2, 20, 48, 56-58, 65 note 9, 86, 95, 111, 116

Printed in Great Britain
by Amazon